Where to Find that Job

Alan Bartlett

Moving Ahead Series

HOBSONS

CRAC

Acknowledgments

Alan Bartlett and Hobsons Publishing PLC would like to record their gratitude to Joseph Clarke, publisher of *Where to Look for Job Vacancies*, for his co-operation during the preparation of this book.

© Hobsons Publishing PLC 1994

ISBN 1 85324 932 7

A CIP record for this book is available from the British Library.

No part of this publication may be copied or reproduced, stored in any retrieval system or transmitted in any form or by any means electronic or mechanical or by photocopying, recording or otherwise without prior permission of the publishers.

CRAC

The Careers Research and Advisory Centre (CRAC) is a registered educational charity. Hobsons Publishing PLC produces CRAC publications under exclusive licence and royalty agreements.

Cover design by Jane Norman

Printed and bound in Great Britain by Clays Ltd, St Ives plc
Typeset by MFK Typesetting Ltd, Hitchin, Hertfordshire.

Ref. L194/E/5/qq/L/JE

Contents

Introduction 1
The purpose of this handbook
How to use this book

1 How to Choose and Apply for Jobs

1 Assessing Yourself and Your Progress 5
The purpose of this chapter
Assessing and recording what you have to offer
Deciding what you want from the job
Wanting to return to paid employment?
Your next steps

2 Careers and Educational Choice 15
The purpose of this chapter
Who needs guidance?
What can you expect from this guidance?
Who provides vocational guidance for adults?
Other ways of getting information about specific careers
Annex 1: Professional and Examining Bodies

3 Vocational Education and Training 44
The purpose of this chapter
Why we need lifetime learning
What the government is doing
Who provides vocational education?
Financial help

4 Job-hunting is a Job in Itself — 54
The purpose of this chapter
Organising your job hunt
Using personal contacts
Making speculative approaches
Identifying potential employers
Reviewing your job-hunting programme

5 Alternative Ways of Working — 66
The purpose of this chapter
Reasons for the growth in self-employment
Would self-employment suit me?
Agencies to help you to decide
Financial help, advice and training
Franchising
Co-operatives
Part-time working
Job-sharing
Annex 2: Names and Addresses of TECs and LECs

2 How Employers Recruit their Staff

Introduction: Where to Find Job Vacancies — 93

6 Jobcentres, Recruitment Agencies and Consultants — 96
The purpose of this chapter
Jobcentres
Recruitment agencies
Employment bureaux
Recruitment consultants
Headhunters

7 Using the Media 105
  The purpose of this chapter
  Finding your way around the national press
  Finding out about jobs in other areas
  How to find jobs in your region
  Trade, professional and other periodicals
  BBC television and radio
  Independent television

8 Vacancies Abroad 123
  The purpose of this chapter
  Why work abroad?
  The implications of working abroad
  Answering these questions
  Working in the European Community
  Specific job opportunities
  Seasonal and casual work abroad

9 Graduate Vacancies 135
  The purpose of this chapter
  Graduate unemployment
  What major graduate employers offer
  How to find out about potential employers
  Not sure what you want to do?
  Know what you want but can't get it?

10 Quick Reference Guide: Job Advertisements in the Press 145
  The purpose of this chapter
  An alphabetical list of over 300 occupations and over 200 publications in which vacancies in these fields are advertised

Introduction

The purpose of this handbook

This book is written for adults who are looking for work or considering a change of job.

It is designed to increase your employment prospects by helping you to find your way through the maze of information that is now available about jobs and related issues – and to enable you to select and use it to your best advantage.

Since the early 1980s a whole industry has grown up around the fact that, because of fundamental changes in the nature of employment, job-hunting is no longer a straightforward matter. To use a cliché, 'job-hunting has become a job in itself'. As a result, a vast range of information and other help is now available to enable job-hunting to be undertaken successfully – through government-funded schemes, newspapers, specialist journals, radio, television or other sources.

It is important for your success in finding work that you are able to make sense of and exploit these resources. This book can help you to do this quickly and systematically.

How to use this book

This is a practical handbook designed to help you quickly locate your particular job information needs. It is divided into two parts.

You will want to refer to Part 1 if you need help identifying your skills or if you are not sure what kind of job to apply for. Part 1 also includes information on working for yourself and an overview of the work-related education and training system.

Part 2 will enable you to identify the sources of actual and potential job vacancies in your chosen field of work. It includes information on graduate opportunities and working abroad. For easy reference, it also contains an alphabetical list of around 300 occupations and the titles of over 200 publications in which vacancies for such occupations are regularly advertised.

1

How to Choose and Apply for Jobs

1 Assessing Yourself and Your Progress

The purpose of this chapter

This chapter helps you to decide what you have to offer to employers and what you want from your job. It provides tips on how you can record this information for use in your job applications and explains what you need to do next.

It is also intended to help you to decide what you could do next if you have spent a period away from paid employment, for example, because you have been involved in full-time domestic activities, serving a custodial sentence or incapacitated through ill health.

Assessing and recording what you have to offer

You can start this process by drawing up a chart similar to the one on the next page. In this case, you use the left-hand column to record details of your education and training, employment and interests/activities outside work. You then use the right-hand columns to record your answers to the questions posed.

This is likely to be quite a time-consuming exercise. It should, however, prove to be cost-effective as you will be able to use what you record as the substance for all your subsequent job applications. This does not mean that the information will remain the same – looking at job advertisements, for example, is almost certain to prompt you to remember other things you have done but had forgotten about. Although not essential, it will clearly be an advantage if you are able to use a word processor to keep this information up to date and adapt it to fit particular vacancy needs.

	What did I do?	What responsibility/ authority did I have?	Achievements	What did I enjoy most and least?
Education and training				
Employment: (show last first, including name, business, size)				
Interests/ activities				

It is vital that, in drawing up your list, you take account of every possible asset you have to offer to a prospective employer. More will be said about this later in the section on writing job applications.

Deciding what you want from the job

Job content

You will probably be able to decide from the information you drew up in the previous section where your strengths and experiences lie and what sorts of job activities you prefer.

Status

The information you recorded will also help you to decide what level of responsibility you want and are capable of holding – whether you are more inclined towards personal performance or towards managing and leading others, or maybe an equal balance of the two; whether your qualifications enable you to operate in a professional advisory capacity or to be a manager with responsibility for other staff.

Salary

You will want to consider what is the minimum salary package you would be able and willing to accept, given your financial commitments. Try to compare this, as far as possible, with rates offered in the advertisements. Not all adverts quote the salary, however, and you may be able to negotiate a better package – it will depend, of course, on the market and what you have to sell. What you are prepared to accept will almost inevitably be influenced by your current employment status.

Mobility

You will need to decide whether you are prepared to move to other areas to work. This is obviously something you would need to discuss with others who would be closely affected by any such decision.

Prospects

You will want to consider how ambitious you are at this stage – whether you are looking for a job with further prospects of advancement and whether, for example, you would be prepared to relocate to secure promotion.

Wanting to return to paid employment?

If you have not been in paid employment for some time the task of finding work can be daunting. There are, however, a number of agencies that can help. For example, women returning to work, ex-offenders and people with disabilities (as well as ex-servicemen and women) have priority when applying for the services provided by Jobcentres and for Training for Work schemes delivered by Training and Enterprise Councils (TECs) in England and Wales and Local Enterprise Companies (LECs) in Scotland. You can join these schemes as soon as you register as unemployed. Jobcentres also provide a specialist resettlement service for people with disabilities.

Women returners

There are a number of organisations to help women to return to work, to education and to jobs in which women traditionally have been under-represented such as science and technology. New Opportunities for Women (NOW) and Wider Opportunities for Women (WOW) offer access to further and higher education, from 'taster' and introductory part-time courses (such as Learning Links) to certificated year-long courses in technology and career development. Every course includes elements of personal and career development, from assertiveness and basic mathematics or study skills to management, training and company placements.

One of the key organisations is the Women Returners' Network which promotes women's re-entry to the labour force through education, training and employment opportunities. The Women Returners' Network is also knowledgeable about NOW and WOW programmes funded by the European Social Fund. For details of your nearest scheme in England and Wales, write to them at:

Women Returners' Network
8 John Adam Street
London W2 6EA
Tel: 0171-839 8188
Fax: 0171-839 5805

For details of schemes in Scotland, write to:

Training 2000
St George's Studios
93–97 St George's Road
Glasgow G3 6JA
Tel: 0141-332 2884

The Women Returners' Network also works closely with TECs so it's worth getting in touch with your local TEC to see what help it can provide.

☛ the list of addresses of TECs/LECs is on pages 81–90.

People with disabilities

If you have been sick or have suffered injuries that mean you can no longer follow your previous occupation, or are looking for work for the first time, there are a number of steps you can take to prepare yourself for a job. You could:

▶ take a course at a college of further or higher education, with whatever extra help may be available from the college, the local authority and voluntary organisations
▶ take up training under one of the programmes arranged by your local TEC (in England and Wales) or LEC (in Scotland)
▶ use more flexible education schemes which enable you to learn at home, for example with the Open University
▶ do a course specifically designed for people with disabilities and run by one of the specialist colleges or organisations.

For further information, contact the Disability Employment Adviser at your local Jobcentre who will be able to advise you about what is available. The adviser might be able to provide assistance to your past employer to retain your services or to help a new employer with employment costs. If you are severely disabled, he or she will also be able to tell you about the opportunities to work in a sheltered environment, including Remploy factories, or alongside able-bodied people in open industry (when a subsidy is paid to the employer to cover part of the wages costs).

You can ring your Jobcentre to make an appointment with the Disability Employment Adviser and/or contact your local TEC/LEC to see what courses they provide.

If you want to find out about courses offered by the Open University, contact:

The Office for Students with Disabilities
The Open University
Walton Hall
Milton Keynes
Buckinghamshire MK7 6AA
Tel: 01908 653442

The following publications are specifically intended to help people with disabilities get back into work and/or training:

Directory for Disabled People, compiled by Ann Darnborough and Derek Kinrad, published by Woodhead Faulkner in association with the Royal Association for Disability and Rehabilitation (RADAR).
A handbook of information and opportunities. A new edition is available from October 1994 from RADAR, priced £22 plus postage and packing or from bookshops.

Training for disabled people; Working with disabled people; Working from home; Guidelines for policy on employment of disabled people
A series of four leaflets published by RADAR, priced 75p each.

Employment Rights: a guide for disabled people
Also available from RADAR, priced £3.50 plus postage and packing.

For information about these and other relevant publications and general employment issues, contact:

RADAR
12 City Forum
250 City Road
London EC1B 8AF
Tel: 0171-250 3222

There is an employment bureau that deals specifically with disabled people. For further information, contact:

Opportunities for people with disabilities
74 Great Portland Street
London W1N 5AL
Tel: 0171-580 7545

Ex-offenders

One important thing to bear in mind if you're thinking of returning to education is that you are likely to experience very little, if any, prejudice from the colleges.

If you are returning to work after a custodial sentence, there are a number of organisations that will help you to re-establish yourself in work, education and training. These include the National Association for the Care and Resettlement of Offenders (NACRO). They have New Careers Training Centres throughout England and Wales which offer full-time adult and/or youth training in a wide range of jobs and in basic skills such as literacy and numeracy. They can also offer employment advice. Some centres run Jobclubs for ex-offenders. For further information, contact:

NACRO Information Department
169 Clapham Road
London SW9 0PU
Tel: 0171-582 6500

NACRO's National Education Advisory Service can provide information and advice on education and training courses and colleges throughout England and Wales and can help you with applying for grants and loans. Contact:

NACRO National Education Advisory Service
567a Barlow Moor Road
Chorlton-cum-Hardy
Manchester M21 2AE
Tel: 0161-861 9737

The Scottish Association for the Care and Resettlement of Offenders can be contacted at:

National Office
SACRO
31 Palmerston Place
Edinburgh EH12 5AP
Tel: 0131-226 4222

The Apex Trust works nationally to improve the employment prospects for ex-offenders. It operates 30 training centres nationwide which offer a range of skills relating to the needs of local labour markets. It also operates Jobclubs throughout the UK which can provide training in job-seeking techniques, and runs a job placement and advice service for ex-offenders and serving prisoners. The Apex Trust can be contacted at:

Apex Trust
1–4 Brixton Hill Place
London SW2 1HL
Tel: 0181-671 7633

The Bridgebuilders Association for the education and guidance of offenders has contacts in most parts of England and Wales. They can give information on education and training available locally and nationally, advice on where and how to apply for grants and help with interview and job-hunting skills. Get in touch with them at:

Bridgebuilders NDU
Robins Wood House
Robins Wood Road
Nottingham NG8 3NH
Tel: 01602 293291
Fax: 01602 299392

Don't underestimate yourself
If you haven't been in paid employment for some time it is easy to underestimate your abilities. But just think, for example, of the range of skills you need to run a house. Now consider how you could apply these to paid work. For example, you probably had to do all or most of the following:

- budget your money
- care for, counsel and teach your children
- undertake household tasks such as decorating
- care for the sick and/or elderly
- look after a garden
- drive a car.

These are all things that other people earn their living by, so why not you? You may, of course, have to do some training to back up your practical experience but not necessarily. It may be possible to get some formal recognition for your skills through National Vocational Qualifications and a system known as Accreditation of Prior Learning (APL).

Your next steps

If you are not sure what you want to do next, ☛ chapter 2 for advice on jobs, education and training.

If you're thinking of going to college or re-training, ☛ chapter 3 for ideas about how you could use the education and training system to improve your prospects.

If you know what you want to do and are already qualified to do it, ☛ chapter 4 for tips on organising a job hunt.

If you're thinking about whether to work for yourself, ☛ chapter 5 for information about alternative ways of working.

2 Careers and Educational Choice

The purpose of this chapter

If you're not sure what you want to do in future, or feel that your employment prospects may be enhanced by obtaining further qualifications, this chapter tells you where you might find advice about careers and vocational education and training. It also explains what sort of help you might expect to get.

It will become clear that whilst there are many organisations that give careers and educational advice/guidance to adults, none of them is equipped to provide guidance to all adults throughout the country. Furthermore, some of the major providers, like the Careers Service and the Adult Educational Guidance Service, are undergoing radical organisational changes and/or are fundamentally affected by a shortage of cash.

Who needs guidance?

You may need careers and/or educational guidance if you are:

- ▶ entering the labour market for the first time
- ▶ returning to paid employment after a break
- ▶ facing an enforced change of occupation
- ▶ voluntarily seeking a change of career.

What can you expect from this guidance?

The National Association for Educational Guidance for Adults and the Institute of Careers Guidance recommend that the guidance provided for adults by the Careers and Educational Guidance Services should enable you to:

- make realistic decisions about your next step
- understand and assess the available opportunities (in jobs and education)
- assess your own potential
- choose widely from all the options open to you
- make and implement an agreed plan of action.

This is therefore what you could hope to expect from your local Educational Guidance Service, if there is one, or from your local Careers Service if they have the means to provide one-to-one counselling for adults.

Who provides vocational guidance for adults?

The Careers Service

Present provision for adults

The Careers Service is the main public provider of careers guidance. As an adult, you may be able to obtain individual vocational counselling from your local Careers Service. It depends on where you live. Under the control of the local education authorities (LEAs), some areas, like Birmingham, Coventry and Sheffield, offer an all-age guidance service; in other parts of the country, counselling for adults is only available if you have been in full-time education during the last two years. In some areas the Careers Service is offered in conjunction with the Educational Guidance Service for Adults.

Future provision for adults

The government is currently offering up the provision of the Careers Service to open tender. The introduction of new management has been planned to occur in three phases – in April 1994, 1995 and 1996. The pattern of bidding for the first tranche in April 1994 was such that the LEAs have continued to be involved in the provision of the service in all those 13 areas, mainly in partnership with the TECs.

The Secretary of State for Scotland has invited the Local Enterprise Companies (LECs) and the LEAs to tender jointly to provide the Careers Service in Scotland from April 1995.

As an adult, you will only have a statutory right to use the Careers Service if you are:

▶ undertaking full-time education of any kind or part-time education related to work other than in an institution of higher education (in which case you would be expected to use the careers service in your college)
▶ under 21 and left education or full-time training less than two years ago
▶ registered as having a disability, including learning difficulties.

Some areas may, however, be better off under the new funding system and will have the discretion to extend the range of eligibility to other adult groups. You may be charged a fee but may receive help with this through the Gateways to Learning or Skill Choice schemes (see below).

How much does it cost?

Hampshire TEC operates the Directions Scheme (another name for Skill Choice) and uses the Careers Services of both Hampshire and Surrey and a dozen private consultants. With one exception, these 14 organisations all charge about £70 for a careers advisory interview lasting for about one and a half hours and a similar amount for any subsequent counselling sessions, if required. Psychometric testing is also available at a cost of £105.

The TEC contributes £30 to the cost of each of the first and any subsequent interviews and £50 for psychometric testing; you pay the rest. Everyone is entitled to a free 15-minute diagnostic session with the advisory agency before committing themselves to paying for the service. Exceptionally in this group of providers, one of the private consultants charges up to £5,000 but this would cover the whole range of services described in the section on Counselling after redundancy. This service is mainly intended for people in employment.

☛ the section on Private providers of vocational guidance.

What other help can the Careers Service give?

You may be able to use the careers library and/or other facilities so it's worth contacting your local Careers Service to see what it can do for you. You can contact your local Careers Service direct, or through your local TEC or LEC. The addresses and telephone numbers of TECs and LECs are given in the annex to chapter 5.

The Educational Guidance Service for Adults

The Educational Guidance Service for Adults is used by over 300,000 people each year. Although the two services are financed by different blocks of money, the aims of the Guidance Service are essentially similar to those of the Careers Service. Many adult education guidance centres are therefore run in conjunction with the Careers Service or as partnerships between local authorities and TECs.

Each centre has information about the range of local education provision. Additionally, advisers are usually available to enable you to make sense of the options and to provide individual guidance on education, training and careers. They should be able to advise you about study fees and other costs, and the availability of grants and other financial support. Some centres offer computer-assisted careers guidance, aptitude assessments, such as psychometric testing, and careers counselling.

Like the Careers Service, the level of provision is affected by financial constraints and varies from area to area. The policy for charging direct fees varies markedly and each service is able to exercise considerable discretion in how it prices its services. There is no statutory obligation to provide a free service and, although in some areas the service is free to all, more authorities are likely to be forced into charging for at least part of the service.

In practice, up to now the basic information service has been free to anyone dropping into a centre. You are more likely to be charged for one-to-one guidance and counselling, particularly if you are currently employed. You may, however, be eligible for one of the schemes operated by the TECs to provide free or subsidised guidance for adults. Information about local provision of educational guidance should be available from your local library, Jobcentre or TEC.

The Further Education Unit has also generously offered to provide copies of its *Directory of Educational Guidance Services for Adults*. It points out, however, that this may quickly be out of date as things are changing rapidly. The directory can be obtained from:

The Further Education Unit
Citadel Place
Tinworth Street
London SE11 5EH
Tel: 0171-962 1280

Computer-based education information services

If you are looking for information about specific courses there are a number of computerised databases that can give you rapid access to this information.

Training Access Points (TAPs)

Training Access Points provide readily accessible computerised information on education and training providers including colleges, private organisations and chambers of commerce. TAPs are located in various establishments, for example, public libraries, careers offices and Jobcentres. Look in the telephone directory or contact your local library, Jobcentre or careers office for your nearest TAP.

ECCTIS 2000 (Education Counselling and Credit Transfer Information Service)

ECCTIS 2000 is a national computerised service which carries information on around 100,000 courses in over 700 universities and colleges of higher and further education throughout the country. It enables you to feed in your requirements and then provides information about the courses that match your needs, including the course title, duration, mode of study (full- or part-time), qualifications awarded, entry requirements, address and telephone number of the institute and details about the course structure and content. Details of educational credit accumulation and transfer schemes (CATS) in higher education institutes are also given.

☛ chapter 3 for an explanation of the educational credit accumulation and transfer scheme.

ECCTIS is available in over 3,500 schools, universities, colleges, libraries, TECs and TAPs throughout the country. Ask your local library, Careers Service or Jobcentre where the nearest one to you is located.

Training and Enterprise Councils and Local Enterprise Companies

Training and Enterprise Councils (TECs) in England and Wales, and Local Enterprise Companies (LECs) in Scotland, were set up by the government to provide a local focus for training and employment initiatives. Since their inception, TECs and LECs have become increasingly involved in educational and careers guidance and some have set up high street shops to provide information about vocational education, training, careers and self-employment. In addition, some are involved in the delivery of the Department of Employment initiatives Gateways to Learning and Skill Choice which encourage individuals to seek educational and careers guidance.

You can contact your local TEC or LEC direct to find out what it provides.

☛ the list of addresses and telephone numbers in the annex to chapter 5.

Gateways to Learning

At the time of writing, a selection of TECs are involved in developing the Gateways to Learning programme. This is a scheme whereby vouchers are given to adults to enable them to buy guidance from local providers (including the Careers and Adult Educational Guidance Services). TECs have the freedom to decide who qualifies but in practice preference is likely to be given to people who have been long-term unemployed, women returning to the labour market after bringing up children and recently redundant workers. It is expected that all TECs will eventually operate a scheme to encourage adults to seek guidance in this way.

For example, SoloTEC, the South London Training and Enterprise Council, operates this scheme under the title of Passport to Work. Vouchers worth up to £70 are given to local people who have been unemployed for over six months to get professional advice and vocational guidance. These can be 'spent' at any one of 12 local agencies including the Careers and Adult Educational Guidance Services and private sector careers consultants.

Skill Choice

Skill Choice is also operated by TECs, mainly for people

already in employment. It is designed to encourage individuals to seek guidance to enable them to make 'effective decisions about future career and learning needs'. Participants are given a proportion of the total cost of guidance and assessment services. This can include the Careers Service and the Adult Educational Guidance Service.

☞ the section on How much does it cost?

Counselling after redundancy

Outplacement is the term given to counselling and careers advice provided to redundant staff by their former employer. The service includes professional counselling to help individuals to cope with redundancy, assess their strengths and weaknesses and prepare for change. It might also cover careers guidance and help with job-hunting techniques. It is possible for you as an individual to pay for this service but the cost is likely to be substantial. For information about these services, send a stamped, self-addressed envelope to:

The Counselling at Work Division (CAWD)
British Association for Counselling
1 Regents Close
Rugby
Warwickshire CV21 2PJ

Private providers of vocational guidance

Private providers of vocational guidance counselling have proliferated during recent years, primarily in response to corporate demand for redundancy counselling. They also provide a service to individuals. The fees are likely to be substantial so, before committing yourself, tell them what your needs are and find out exactly what they think they can do to help you. Your first step might be to obtain their brochures. Two long established providers of full psychological assessment, testing and counselling are:

Career Analysts
Career House
90 Gloucester Place
London W1H 4BL
Tel: 0171-935 5452

Vocational Guidance Association
7 Harley House
Upper Harley Street
London NW1 4RP
Tel: 0171-935 2600

☛ the section on How much does it cost?

Careers advice for women

The Career Development Centre for Women (CDC4W) offers career and life planning programmes for individuals. A nominal fee is payable for an initial interview that lasts for about an hour. A further fee would then be payable if you decided to follow a programme. Details can be obtained from:

CDC4W
97 Mallard Place
Strawberry Vale
Twickenham
Middlesex TW1 4SW
Tel: 0181-892 3806

☛ the section on Women returners in chapter 1.

Other providers of advice

Colleges and universities

As part of their policy to respond more closely to the needs of the local economy, further education colleges are now expected to offer advice to potential students about the vocational relevance of courses. In many instances this is likely to be confined to the courses offered by the particular college. In others it will include information about provision in other local educational establishments, whilst some will have the resources to offer advice on wider issues of career planning. If you are considering undertaking a course at FE level it is worth contacting your local FE college to find out what help they can give.

Most universities are now keen to talk to potential mature students and in some instances will refer you to their careers advisers if you are unsure about the qualifications required for a particular career. Contact your local university to find out what they can do for you.

☛ the section on higher education in chapter 3 and the information about graduate vacancies in chapter 9.

Other ways of getting information about specific careers

Careers literature

If you are looking for information about specific careers you will probably want to turn first to one of several careers compendia, such as *Occupations* which is published annually by the Careers and Occupational Information Centre. These provide an overview of entry qualifications and other requirements, including opportunities for adult entry, what the work and conditions and prospects for promotion are like and where the jobs are likely to be. If you see something that interests you, you may find other publications that concentrate on that particular occupation or industry. In careers libraries you will also find 'wallets' of information on specific careers including the information provided by the professional and industry bodies.

Some careers offices now have 'microDOORS' – an occupational information database, on computer, covering over 1,000 job titles. This will enable you to match your skills and interests to jobs and will provide you with printouts of information on the jobs that interest you.

Professional bodies

Information about careers can be obtained from the respective professional bodies and institutes.

☞ the list of professional bodies in the annex to this chapter.

Annex 1: Professional and Examining Bodies

Information about careers can be obtained from the respective professional bodies and institutes. These are listed below in alphabetical order of profession.

Accountancy

The Association of Accounting Technicians
154 Clerkenwell Road
London EC1R 5AD

Association of Cost and Executive Accountants
149 Fonthill Road
London N4 3HF

The Association of International Accountants
South Bank Building
Kingsway Team Valley
Gateshead
Tyne and Wear NE11 0JS

The Chartered Association of Certified Accountants
29 Lincoln's Inn Fields
London WC2A 3EE

The Chartered Association of Certified Accountants: Scottish Branch
2 Woodside Place
Glasgow G3 7QF

The Chartered Institute of Management Accountants
63 Portland Place
London W1N 4AB

The Institute of Chartered Accountants in England and Wales
PO Box 433
Chartered Accountants' Hall
Moorgate Place
London EC2P 2BJ

The Institute of Chartered Accountants in Ireland
Scottish Amicable House
11 Donegal Square South
Belfast BT1 5JE

The Institute of Chartered Accountants of Scotland
27 Queen Street
Edinburgh EH2 1LA

The Institute of Financial Accountants
Burford House
44 London Road
Sevenoaks
Kent TN13 1AS

The Institute of Internal Auditors
13 Abbeville Mews
88 Clapham Park Road
London SW4 7BX

International Association of Book-keepers
Burford House
44 London Road
Sevenoaks
Kent TN13 1AS

Acoustics
Institute of Acoustics
Agriculture House
5 Holywell Hill
St Albans
Hertfordshire AL1 1EU

Administration
The Institute of Administrative Management
40 Chatsworth Parade
Petts Wood
Orpington
Kent BR5 1RW

The Institute of Chartered Secretaries and Administrators
16 Park Crescent
London W1N 4AH

Advertising
The Communication, Advertising and Marketing Education Foundation
Abford House
15 Wilton Road
London SW1V 1NJ

Institute of Practitioners in Advertising
44 Belgrave Square
London SW1X 8QS

Aeronautics
Royal Aeronautical Society
4 Hamilton Place
London W1V 0BQ

Agriculture/ Arboriculture/ Horticulture/ Viticulture
National Examinations Board for Agriculture, Horticulture and Allied Industries
46 Britannia Street
London WC1X 9RG

The Royal Forestry Society of England, Wales and Northern Ireland
102 High Street
Tring
Hertfordshire HP23 4AF

Royal Horticultural Society
Royal Horticultural Society's Garden
Wisley
Woking
Surrey GU23 6QB

Royal Scottish Forestry Society
62 Queen Street
Edinburgh EH2 4NA

Wine and Spirit Education Trust
Five Kings House
1 Queen Street Place
London EC4R 1QS

Animal Technology
The Institute of Animal Technology
5 South Parade
Summertown
Oxford OX2 7JL

Architecture
The Architects' and Surveyors' Institute
15 St Mary Street
Chippenham
Wiltshire SN15 3JN

British Institute of Architectural Technicians
397 City Road
London EC1V 1NE

Royal Institute of British Architects
66 Portland Place
London W1N 4AD

Auctioneering
Incorporated Society of
  Valuers and Auctioneers
3 Cadogan Gate
London SW1X 0AS

Audiology
British Association of
  Audiological Physicians
The Royal Surrey County
  Hospital
Egerton Road
Guildford GU2 5XX

British Association of
  Audiological Scientists
c/o British Society of
  Audiology
80 Brighton Road
Reading RG6 1PS

Aviation
Civil Aviation Authority
CAA House
45–59 Kingsway
London WC2B 6TE

Banking
The Chartered Institute of
  Bankers
10 Lombard Street
London EC3V 9AS

The Chartered Institute of
  Bankers in Scotland
19 Rutland Square
Edinburgh EH1 2DE

Beauty Therapy
Confederation of Beauty
  Therapy and Cosmetology
2nd Floor
34 Imperial Square
Cheltenham
Gloucestershire GL50 1QZ

International Health and
  Beauty Council
46 Aldwick Road
Bognor Regis
West Sussex PO21 2PN

Society of Cosmetic Scientists
GT House
24–26 Rothesay Road
Luton
Bedfordshire LU1 1QX

Bee-keeping
British Bee-keepers'
  Association
26 Coldharbour Lane
Hildenborough
Tonbridge
Kent TN11 9JT

Biology/Biomedicine
Biological Engineering Society
c/o Royal College of Surgeons
31–43 Lincoln's Inn Fields
London WC2A 3PN

Institute of Biology
20 Queensberry Place
London SW7 2DZ

Institute of Biomedical Science
12 Coldbath Square
London EC1R 5HL

Bookselling
Booksellers' Association of
  Great Britain and Ireland
Minister House
272 Vauxhall Bridge Road
London SW1V 1BA

Brewing
The Institute of Brewing
33 Clarges Street
London W1Y 8EE

Building

Association of Building Engineers
Jubilee House
Billing Brook Road
Weston Favell
Northampton NN3 4NW

The Chartered Institute of Building
Englemere
Kings Ride
Ascot
Berkshire SL5 8BJ

The Chartered Institute of Housing
Octavia House
Westwood Business Park
Westwood Way
Coventry CV4 8JP

The Chartered Institution of Building Services Engineers
Delta House
222 Balham High Road
London SW12 9BS

The Institute of Building Control
21 High Street
Ewell
Epsom
Surrey KT17 1SB

Institute of Clerks of Works of Great Britain Inc.
41 The Mall
Ealing
London W5 3TJ

Business

The Association of Business Executives
William House
14 Worple Road
Wimbledon
London SW19 4DD

Department of Trade and Industry
43 Bartholomew Close
London EC1A 7HP

Institute of Business Administration
25 Bridgeman Terrace
Wigan
Lancashire WN1 1TD

Cardiology

Society of Cardiological Technicians
2 Poplar Avenue
Windlesham
Surrey GU20 6PL

Society of Cardiological Technicians (Northern Ireland)
15 Milfort Avenue
Dunmurry
Belfast BT17 9BJ

Carpentry

The Institute of Carpenters
Central Office
35 Hayworth Road
Sandiacre
Nottingham NG10 5LL

Carpet Fitters

National Institute of Carpet Fitters
4D St Mary's Place
The Lace Market
Nottingham NG1 1PH

Charitable Organisations

British Red Cross Society
9 Grosvenor Crescent
London SW1X 7EJ

The Royal Life Saving Society UK
Mountbatten House
Studley
Warwickshire B80 7NN

St Andrew's Ambulance
   Association
St Andrew's House
48 Milton Street
Glasgow G4 0HR

St John Ambulance
   Association
1 Grosvenor Crescent
London SW1X 7EF

Chemistry
Oil and Colour Chemists'
   Association
Priory House
967 Harrow Road
Wembley
Middlesex HA0 2SF

Royal Society of Chemistry
Burlington House
Piccadilly
London W1V 0BN

Society of Apothecaries
Apothecaries' Hall
Blackfriars Lane
London EC4V 6EJ

Childcare
Council for Awards in
   Children's Care and
   Education
8 Chequer Street
St Albans
Hertfordshire AL1 3XZ

National Association for
   Maternal and Child Welfare
40–42 Osnaburgh Street
London NW1 3ND

Chiropody/Podiatry
Society of Chiropodists and
   Podiatrists
53 Welbeck Street
London W1M

Computing/Data Processing
Association of Business and
   Administrative Computing
William House
14 Worple Road
Wimbledon
London SW19 4DD

Association of Computer
   Professionals
204 Barnett Wood Lane
Ashtead
Surrey KT21 2DB

British Computer Society
PO Box 1454
Station Road
Swindon SN1 1TG

The Institute of Data
   Processing Management
IDPM House
Edgington Way
Ruxley Corner
Sidcup
Kent DA14 5HR

Dentistry
Association of British Dental
   Surgery Assistants
DSA House
29 London Street
Fleetwood
Lancashire FY7 6JY

General Dental Council
37 Wimpole Street
London W1M 8DQ

Designers
Chartered Society of Designers
29 Bedford Square
London WC1B 3EG

Society of Designer-Craftsmen
24 Rivington Street
London EC2A 3DU

Dietetics
The British Dietetic
 Association
7th Floor, Elizabeth House
22 Suffolk Street
Queensway
Birmingham B1 1LS

Display
British Display Society
70a Crayford High Street
Dartford
Kent DA1 4EF

Distribution
Institute of Grocery
 Distribution
Grange Lane
Letchmore Heath
Watford
Hertfordshire WD2 8DQ

Energy
The Institute of Energy
18 Devonshire Street
London W1N 2AU

Engineering
The Engineering Council
10 Maltravers Street
London WC2R 3ER

The Institute of Asphalt
 Technology
Unit 18
Central Trading Estate
Staines
Middlesex TW18 4XE

Institute of Automotive
 Engineer Assessors
Mansell House
22 Bore Street
Lichfield
Staffordshire WS13 6LP

Institute of Highway
 Incorporated Engineers
20 Queensberry Place
London SW7 2DR

Institute of Hospital
 Engineering
2 Abingdon House
Cumberland Business Centre
Northumberland Road
Portsmouth PO5 1DS

Institute of Incorporated
 Executive Engineers
Wix Hill House
West Horsley
Surrey KT24 6DZ

The Institute of Marine
 Engineers
The Memorial Building
76 Mark Lane
London EC3R 7JN

Institute of Road Transport
 Engineers
1 Cromwell Place
London SW7 2JF

Institute of Sheet Metal
 Engineering
Exeter House
48 Holloway Head
Birmingham B1 1NQ

The Institution of Agricultural
 Engineers
West End Road
Silsoe
Bedfordshire MK45 4DU

Institution of Chemical
 Engineers
Davis Building
165–189 Railway Terrace
Rugby
Warwickshire CV21 3HQ

The Institution of Civil
   Engineers
1–7 Great George Street
Westminster
London SW1P 3AA

The Institution of Electrical
   Engineers
Savoy Place
London WC2R 0BL

The Institution of Electronics
   and Electrical Incorporated
   Engineers
Savoy Hill House
Savoy Hill
London WC2R 0BS

The Institution of Engineering
   Designers
Courtleigh
Westbury Leigh
Westbury
Wiltshire BA13 3TA

Institution of Engineers and
   Shipbuilders in Scotland
1 Atlantic Quay
Bloomfield
Glasgow G2 8JE

The Institution of Gas
   Engineers
21 Portland Place
London W1N 3AF

The Institution of Lighting
   Engineers
Lennox House
9 Lawford Road
Rugby
Warwickshire CV21 2DZ

The Institution of Mechanical
   Engineers
Northgate Avenue
Bury St Edmunds
Suffolk IP32 6BN

The Institution of Mechanical
   Incorporated Engineers
3 Birdcage Walk
Westminster
London SW1H 9JN

Institution of Nuclear
   Engineers
Allan House
1 Penerley Road
London SE6 2LQ

The Institution of Plant
   Engineers
77 Great Peter Street
London SW1P 2EZ

The Institution of Structural
   Engineers
11 Upper Belgrave Street
London SW1X 8BH

English Language Teaching

Association of Recognised
   English Language Schools
   (ARELS) Examinations
Ewert Place
Summertown
Oxford OX2 7BZ

Environmental Health

The Institution of
   Environmental Health
   Officers
Institution of Fire Engineers
148 New Walk
Leicester LE1 7QB

Institution of Water and
   Environmental Management
15 John Street
London WC1N 2EB

Royal Environmental Health
   Institute of Scotland
3 Manor Place
Edinburgh EH3 7DH

Annex 1: Professional and Examining Bodies 33

Equestrianism
The British Horse Society
Examination Office
British Equestrian Centre
Stoneleigh Park
Kenilworth
Warwickshire CV8 2LR

Estate Agents
The National Association of
  Estate Agents
Arbon House
21 Jury Street
Warwick CV34 4EH

Export
The Institute of Export
Export House
64 Clifton Street
London EC2A 4HB

Farriers
The Farriers Registration
  Council
PO Box 49
East of England Showground
Peterborough PE2 6GU

Finance
Association of Consulting
  Actuaries
7 Rolls Building
Fetter Lane
London EC4A 1NH

The Chartered Institute of
  Public Finance and
  Accountancy
3 Robert Street
London WC2N 6BH

The Faculty of Actuaries
23 St Andrew Square
Edinburgh EH2 1AQ

Institute of Actuaries
Napier House
4 Worcester Street
Oxford OX1 2AW

Institute of Credit
  Management
The Water Mill
Station Road
South Luffenham
Oakham
Leicestershire LE15 8NB

Institute of Investment
  Management Research
211–213 High Street
Bromley
Kent BR1 1NY

The Institute of Revenues,
  Rating and Valuation
41 Doughty Street
London WC1N 2LF

The Institute of Taxation
12 Upper Belgrave Street
London SW1X 8BB

The International Stock
  Exchange
Old Broad Street
London EC2N 1HP

The Pensions Management
  Institute
PMI House
Artillery Lane
London E1 7LS

The Securities Institute
Centurion House
24 Monument Street
London EC3 8AJ

Fisheries Management
Institute of Fisheries
  Management
22 Rushworth Avenue
Nottingham NG2 7LF

Floristry
The Society of Floristry Ltd
70a Reigate Road
Epsom
Surrey KT17 3DT

Food Science and Technology
Institute of Food Science and
  Technology
5 Cambridge Court
210 Shepherd's Bush Road
London W6 7NL

The Institute of Meat
Langford
Bristol BS18 7DY

Funeral Services
British Institute of Embalmers
21c Station Road
Knowle
Solihull
West Midlands B93 0HL

Institute of Burial and
  Cremation Administration
  Incorporated
The Gatehouse
Kew Meadow Path
Richmond
Surrey TW9 4EN

Geology
Geological Society
Burlington House
Piccadilly
London W1V 0JU

Glassblowing
British Society of Scientific
  Glassblowers
21 Grebe Avenue
Eccleston Park
St Helens
Merseyside WA10 3QL

Groundsmanship
The Institute of
  Groundsmanship
19–23 Church Street
The Agora
Wolverton
Milton Keynes MK12 5LG

Hairdressing/Trichology
The Hairdressing Training
  Board
3 Chequer Road
Doncaster DN1 2AA

The Incorporated Guild of
  Hairdressers, Wigmakers
  and Perfumers
Syndicate House
27–29 Westgate
Barnsley
South Yorkshire S70 2DJ

The Institute of Trichologists
  Incorporated
228 Stockwell Road
Brixton
London SW9 9SU

History
The Historical Association
59A Kennington Park Road
London SE11 4JH

Home Economics
Institute of Home Economics
Hobart House
40 Grosvenor Place
London SW1X 7AE

Horology
British Horological Institute
Upton Hall
Upton
Newark
Nottinghamshire NG23 5TE

Hotel, Catering and Institutional Management
Hotel, Catering and Institutional Management (HCIMA)
19 Trinity Road
London SW17 7HN

Information Science
Information Systems Examinations Board
7 Mansfield Mews
London W1M 9FJ

The Institute of Information Scientists
44–45 Museum Street
London WC1A 1LY

Innkeeping
The British Institute of Innkeeping
51–53 High Street
Camberley
Surrey GU15 3RG

Insurance
The Chartered Insurance Institute
31 Hillcrest Road
South Woodford
London E18 2JP

Jewellers
National Association of Goldsmiths of Great Britain and Ireland
78a Luke Street
London EC2A 4PY

Journalism
Chartered Institute of Journalists
2 Dock Offices
Surrey Quays Road
London SE16 2XL

National Council for the Training of Broadcast Journalists
188 Litchfield Court
Sheen Road
Richmond TW9 1BB

National Council for the Training of Journalists
Carlton House
Hemhall Street
Epping
Essex CM16 4NL

Periodical Training Council
Imperial House
Kingsway
London WC2B 6UN

Languages
The Institute of Linguists
24A Highbury Grove
London N5 2EA

Law
Council of Legal Education
39 Eagle Street
London WC1R 4AJ

Faculty of Advocates
Advocates' Library
Parliament House
Edinburgh EH1 1RF

The Institute of Legal Executives
Kempston Manor
Kempston
Bedford MK42 7AB

Institute of Paralegal Training
The Mill
Clymping Street
Littlehampton
West Sussex BN17 5RN

The Law Society
227–228 The Strand
London WC2R 1BA

The Law Society of Scotland
26 Drumsheugh Gardens
Edinburgh EH3 7YR

Leisure Management
Institute of Leisure and
  Management
ILAM House
Lower Basildon
Reading
Berkshire RG8 9NE

Institute of Sport and
  Recreation Management
Giffard House
36–38 Sherrard Street
Melton Mowbray
Leicestershire LE13 1XJ

Librarianship
The Library Association
7 Ridgmount Street
London WC1E 7AE

Local Government Management
The Local Government
  Management Board
Arndale House
The Arndale Centre
Luton
Bedfordshire LU1 2TS

Loss Adjusters
The Chartered Institute of
  Loss Adjusters
Manfield House
376 Strand
London WC2R 0LR

Management
The Institute of Health
  Services Management
39 Chalton Street
London NW1 1JD

The Institute of Management
Management House
Cottingham Road
Corby
Northamptonshire NN17 1TT

Institute of Management
  Services
1 Cecil Court
London Road
Enfield
Middlesex EN2 6DD

The Institute of Sales and
  Marketing Management
National Westminster House
31 Upper George Street
Luton
Bedfordshire LU1 2RD

The Institute for Supervision
  and Management
Mansell House
22 Bore Street
Lichfield
Staffordshire WS13 6LP

Methods-Time Management
  Association Ltd
PO Box 20
212 Manchester Road
Warrington
Cheshire WA1 3BD

The National Examining
  Board for Supervisory
  Management
76 Portland Place
London W1N 4AA

Marine Safety
Marine Safety Agency
105 Commercial Road
Southampton
Hampshire SO15 1EG

Marketing
The Chartered Institute of
   Marketing
Moor Hall
Cookham
Maidenhead
Berkshire SL6 9QH

Managing and Marketing Sales
   Association Examination
   Board
PO Box 11
Sandbach
Cheshire CW11 0GD

The Market Research Society
15 Northburgh Street
London EC1V 0AH

Materials Science
Institute of Materials
1 Carlton House Terrace
London SW1Y 5DB

Mathematics
The Institute of Mathematics
   and its Applications
Catherine Richards House
16 Nelson Street
Southend-on-Sea
Essex SS1 1EF

Measurement
The Institute of Measurement
   and Control
87 Gower Street
London WC1E 6AA

Medical Secretaries
The Association of Medical
   Secretaries, Practice
   Administrators and
   Receptionists
Tavistock House
North Tavistock Square
London WC1H 9LN

Metallurgy
Institute of Metal Finishing
Exeter House
48 Holloway Road
Birmingham B1 1NQ

Mining
The Institution of Mining and
   Metallurgy
44 Portland Place
London W1N 4BR

Institution of Mining Electrical
   and Mining Mechanical
   Engineers
60 Silver Street
Doncaster DN1 1HT

Institution of Mining
   Engineers
Danum House
South Parade
Doncaster DN1 2DY

Mining Qualifications Board
Health and Safety Executive
Baynards House
1a Chepstow Place
London W2 4TF

Motor Industry
The Institute of the Motor
   Industry
Fanshaws
Brickendon
Hertford SG13 8PQ

National Joint Council for the
  Motor Vehicle Retail and
  Repair Industry
201 Great Portland Street
London W1N 6AB

Music
Associated Board of the Royal
  Schools of Music
14 Bedford Square
London WC1B 3JG

Guildhall School of Music and
  Drama
Silk Street
Barbican
London EC2Y 8DT

London Academy of Music
  and Dramatic Art
  Examinations
Tower House
226 Cromwell Road
London SW5 0SR

Royal Academy of Music
Marylebone Road
London NW1 5HT

Royal College of Music
Prince Consort Road
London SW7 2BS

The Royal College of Organists
7 St Andrew Street
Holborn
London EC4A 3LQ

Trinity College of Music
Mandeville Place
London W1M 6AQ

Naval Architecture
The Royal Institution of Naval
  Architects
10 Upper Belgrave Street
London SW1X 8BQ

Non-destructive Testing
The British Institute of Non-
  destructive Testing
1 Spencer Parade
Northampton NN1 5AA

Nursing
National Board for Nursing,
  Midwifery and Health
  Visiting for Northern
  Ireland
RAC House
79 Chichester Street
Belfast BT1 4JE

National Board for Nursing,
  Midwifery and Health
  Visiting for Scotland
22 Queen Street
Edinburgh EH2 1JX

Royal College of Nursing of
  the UK
Institute of Advanced Nursing
  Education
20 Cavendish Square
London W1M 0AB

Scottish Nursery Nurses'
  Examination Board
SCOTVEC
Hanover House
24 Douglas Street
Glasgow G2 7NQ

Welsh National Board for
  Nursing, Midwifery and
  Health Visiting
Floor 13, Pearl Assurance
  House
Greyfriars Road
Cardiff CF1 3AG

Occupational Hygiene
British Examining Board in
  Occupational Hygiene
Suite 2, Georgian House
Great Northern Road
Derby DE1 1LT

Occupational Therapy
College of Occupational
  Therapists
6–8 Marshalsea Road
Southwark
London SE1 1HL

Office Systems
British Office Systems and
  Stationery Federation
6 Wimpole Street
London W1M 8AS

Ophthalmology/ Optometry/ Orthoptics
The Association of British
  Dispensing Opticians
6 Hurlingham Business Park
Sullivan Road
London SW6 3DU

The British College of
  Optometrists
10 Knaresborough Place
London SW5 0TG

British Orthoptic Society
Tavistock House
North Tavistock Square
London WC1H 9HX

Osteopathy
The British School of
  Osteopathy
1–4 Suffolk Street
London SW1Y 4HG

Packaging
Institute of Packaging
Sysonby Lodge
Nottingham Road
Melton Mowbray
Leicestershire LE13 0NU

Paper
The National Association of
  Paper Merchants
Hamilton Court
Cogmore Lane
Chertsey
Surrey KT16 9AP

Patenting
The Chartered Institute of
  Patent Agents
Staple Inn Buildings
High Holborn
London WC1V 7PZ

Personnel Management
Institute of Personnel and
  Development
IPD House
35 Camp Road
London SW19 4UX

Pharmaceuticals
The Pharmaceutical Society of
  Northern Ireland
73 University Street
Belfast BT7 1HL

The Royal Pharmaceutical
  Society of Great Britain
1 Lambeth High Street
London SE1 7JN

Photography
British Institute of Professional
  Photography
Amwell End
Ware
Hertfordshire SG12 9HN

The Royal Photographic
  Society
The Octagon
Milsom Street
Bath BA1 1DN

Physical Recreation
Central Council of Physical
  Recreation
Francis House
Francis Street
London SW1P 1DE

Physics
The Institute of Physics
47 Belgrave Square
London SW1X 8QX

Physiotherapy
The Chartered Society of
  Physiotherapy
14 Bedford Row
London WC1R 4ED

Preceptors
The College of Preceptors
Coppice Row
Theydon Bois
Epping
Essex CM16 7DN

Printing
British Printing Industries
  Federation
11 Bedford Row
London WC1R 4DX

Institute of Printing
8 Lonsdale Gardens
Tunbridge Wells
Kent TN1 1NU

Society of Typographic
  Designers
Chapelfield Cottage
Randwick
Stroud
Gloucestershire GL6 6HS

Private Investigators
The Institute of Professional
  Investigators
31a Wellington Street
St Johns
Blackburn BB1 8AF

Production
The British Production and
  Inventory Control Society
The University of Warwick
  Science Park
Sir William Lyons Road
Coventry CV4 7EZ

Psychology
The British Psychological
  Society
St Andrews House
48 Princes Road East
Leicester LE1 7DR

Public Health
The Royal Institute of Public
  Health and Hygiene
28 Portland Place
London W1N 4DE

Public Relations
The Institute of Public
  Relations
The Old Trading House
15 Northburgh Street
London EC1V 0PR

Publishing
Publishers' Association
19 Bedford Square
London WC1B 3HJ

Purchasing
The Chartered Institute of
  Purchasing and Supply
Easton House
Easton-on-the-Hill
Stamford
Lincolnshire PE9 3NZ

Quality Control
Institute of Quality Assurance
PO Box 712
61 Southwark Street
London SE1 1SB

Quarrying
Institute of Quarrying
7 Regent Street
Nottingham NG1 5BS

Radiography
The College of Radiographers
14 Upper Wimpole Street
London W1M 8BN

Safety
Institute of Fire Prevention
   Officers
27 Lurline Gardens
London SW11 4DB

The Institution of
   Occupational Safety and
   Health
The Grange
Highfield Drive
Wigston
Leicester LE18 1NN

Royal Society for the
   Prevention of Accidents
Training Centre
22 Summer Road
Acocks Green
Birmingham B27 7UT

Science
The Association for Science
   Education
College Lane
Hatfield
Hertfordshire AL10 9AA

Institution of Corrosion
   Science and Technology
PO Box 253
Leighton Buzzard
Bedfordshire LU7 7WB

Security
The International Institute of
   Security
IPSA House
3 Dendy Road
Paignton
Devon TQ4 5DB

Shipping
The Institute of Chartered
   Shipbrokers
3 Gracechurch Street
London EC3V 0AT

The Institute of Freight
   Forwarders Ltd
Redfern House
Browells Lane
Feltham
Middlesex TW13 7EP

Social Work
British Association of Social
   Workers
16 Kent Street
Birmingham B5 6RD

Central Council for Education
   and Training in Social Work
Derbyshire House
St Chad's Street
London WC1H 8AD

Institute of Welfare Officers
254 The Corn Exchange
Hanging Ditch
Manchester M4 3BQ

Speech Therapy
The College of Speech and
   Language Therapists
7 Bath Place
Rivington Street
London EC2A 3DR

Sports
Amateur Swimming
 Association
Harold Fern House
Derby Square
Loughborough
Leicestershire LE11 0AL

English Schools' Badminton
 Association
National Badminton Centre
Bradwell Road
Loughton Lodge
Milton Keynes MK8 9LA

The Football Association
16 Lancaster Gate
London W2 3LW

Swimming Teachers
 Association
Anchor House
Birch Street
Walsall
West Midlands WS2 8HZ

Sports Therapy
International Institute of
 Sports Therapy
46 Aldwick Road
Bognor Regis
West Sussex PO21 2PN

Statistics
The Royal Statistical Society
25 Enford Street
London W1H 2BH

Surveyors
The Royal Institution of
 Chartered Surveyors
Surveyor Court
Westwood Way
Coventry CV4 8JE

The Society of Surveying
 Technicians
Surveyor Court
Westwood Way
Coventry CV4 8JE

Taxation
The Association of Taxation
 Technicians
12 Upper Belgrave Street
London SW1X 8BB

Textiles
The Society of Dyers and
 Colourists
PO Box 244
Perkin House
Grattan Road
Bradford
West Yorkshire BD1 2JB

Textile Institute
10 Blackfriars Street
Manchester M3

Therapy
International Therapy
 Examination Council Ltd
James House
Oakelbrook Mill
Newent
Gloucestershire GL18 1HD

Tourism
Confederation of Tourism,
 Hotel and Catering
 Management
204 Barnett Wood Land
Ashtead
Surrey KT21 2DB

Institute of Travel and
 Tourism
113 Victoria Street
St Albans
Hertfordshire AL1 3ST

Town Planning
The Royal Town Planning
  Institute
26 Portland Place
London W1N 4BE

Trading Standards
Institute of Trading Standards
  Administration
4–5 Hadleigh Business Centre
351 London Road
Hadleigh
Essex SS7 2BT

Training
Institute of Training and
  Development
Marlow House
Institute Road
Marlow
Buckinghamshire SL7 1BD

Transport
The Chartered Institute of
  Transport
80 Portland Place
London W1N 4DP

Institute of Transport
  Administration
32 Palmerston Road
Southampton SO1 1LL

Institution of Highways and
  Transportation
3 Lygon Place
Ebury Street
London SW1W 0JS

Veterinary Surgery
Royal College of Veterinary
  Surgeons
32 Belgrave Square
London SW1X 8QP

Wastes Management
Institute of Wastes
  Management
9 Saxon Court
St Peter's Gardens
Northampton NN1 1SX

Welding
The Welding Institute
Abington Hall
Abington
Cambridge CB1 6AL

Wood Science
Institute of Wood Science
Stocking Lane
Hughenden Valley
High Wycombe
Buckinghamshire HP14 4NU

Yachting
Royal Yachting Association
RYA House
Romsey Road
Eastleigh
Hampshire SO50 9YA

Yoga
The British Wheel of Yoga
1 Hamilton Place
Boston Road
Sleaford
Lincolnshire NG34 7ES

3 Vocational Education and Training

The purpose of this chapter

This chapter will help if you are thinking of taking a course to improve your job prospects. It explains why, from now on, people will need to have access to education and training throughout their working lives and describes some of the things that make this possible.

Why we need lifetime learning

In order to compete effectively in future world markets, Britain will need a workforce that is better educated and trained and more highly skilled. Above all, people will need to be more adaptable as it is likely that they will have to make substantive career changes several times during their working lives. This means that education and training must be readily accessible throughout our working lives.

What the government is doing

Training and Enterprise Councils and Local Enterprise Companies

The government set up the Training and Enterprise Councils (TECs) in England and Wales and the Local Enterprise Companies (LECs) in Scotland to give a local emphasis to the delivery of employment, training and enterprise programmes. TECs and LECs are now also required to influence local providers of education, partly through financial incentives and partly through being represented on college management boards.

Training for Work

TECs and LECs are now responsible for the delivery of the

government's training programme for unemployed adults. This is known generically as Training for Work but your local TEC or LEC may have chosen a different title. This programme can take the form of job specific training, work towards a National Vocational Qualification (NVQ), temporary work to keep your skills up to date or a mixture of these options. At the time of writing, participants receive their usual unemployment benefit or income support allowance topped up by £10 per week. Ring your TEC or LEC to find out what it can provide. A list of addresses and telephone numbers is set out in the annex to chapter 5.

National Vocational Qualifications

National Vocational Qualifications (NVQs) concentrate on testing your ability to do the job. In the past, many qualifications have tended to show your knowledge of the theory rather than its practical application. Therefore, depending on the type and level of job, it might be possible to obtain an NVQ by being tested on the job without taking a formal course. In other cases, it might be a combination of this and more formal learning. Because NVQs are split up into modules or units of competences, it is possible to concentrate on the elements that you need rather than include those parts that are not directly relevant to your job just to get the qualification. You can build up your units of competence over a period of time. You will need to provide evidence, which is assessed, for the competences required and this can be done at your workplace or further education college or through Accreditation of Prior Learning (APL).

NVQs are offered by a range of awarding bodies including BTEC, RSA and City and Guilds. They are available at five levels based on the responsibility required in a particular job, ranging from routine to managerial work. In academic terms NVQ level 2 is equivalent to GCE O-levels (now known as GCSEs), level 3 equates to A-levels, and so on. Write to your own professional body or trade association about the availability of NVQs in your line of work, or ask your local FE college what NVQs it offers. A list of the addresses and telephone numbers of the main professional and examining bodies is set out in the annex to chapter 2.

NVQs have not caught on as well as the government would have wished. This is due in part to the fact that people have found that they are not available in their subjects or that there are insufficient qualified people to do the assessment. Nevertheless, NVQs seem to be here to stay and, at the time of writing, the government's target is to have 90 per cent of all occupations covered by NVQs by 1995. Further information about NVQs can be obtained from:

The Publications Department
NCVQ
22 Euston Road
London NW1 2BZ
Tel: 0171-387 9898

Scottish Vocational Qualifications

Scottish Vocational Qualifications are nationally recognised awards designed by the Scottish Vocational Education Council (SCOTVEC) in conjunction with industry and business. They are based on the same principles as NVQs and form part of an overall Scottish framework of qualifications. Further information can be obtained from:

The Marketing Department
SCOTVEC
24 Douglas Street
Glasgow G2 7NG
Tel: 0141-248 7900

Accreditation of Prior Learning

Accreditation of Prior Learning (APL) enables you to

be assessed and credited for what you have learned from previous work and life experience as well as from formal learning. It fits in well with the concept of NVQs, where you don't necessarily have to attend a taught course to get the qualification. If you are interested in studying at a particular institution it's worth finding out whether your previous experience is acceptable for APL.

Who provides vocational education?

Further education colleges

Further education (FE) colleges are the main public providers of vocational education below degree level, such as A-level, BTEC, City and Guilds, or, in NVQ terms, level 3. (See also the section on franchised degrees.) In 1993 the government took these colleges out of the control of local authorities to enable them to respond more flexibly to the needs of individual students and local employers. This means that some FE colleges now provide courses throughout the year, allow you to join a course at any time and provide the studies in modules, making it easier for you to leave off and then take up your course at a later date. It can also mean providing training at your workplace. The government is also expecting FE colleges to be a major provider of NVQs.

However, the extent to which individual colleges have met these challenges varies greatly.

Getting advice about what FE colleges provide

As part of the new regime, FE colleges are required to give advice to potential students on the available courses and their relevance to jobs. Look in your telephone directory or ask your local library where your colleges are located, then ring the college for a brochure. You may want to arrange an appointment to see the student counsellor. In some areas the FE colleges work together, whilst in others they are competitors. In the latter case you may want to compare what each provides.

As well as individual college brochures, there are a number of directories of FE provision which should be available in your local careers library. These include:

The Directory of Further Education published by CRAC
This includes details of over 65,000 courses and of education providers in the UK.

Higher education

Higher education provides studies in a wide range of vocational subjects at first and postgraduate degree level as well as Higher National Diplomas and equivalent levels of professional or vocational education. Degrees are usually studied at a university or college on a full-time basis (including sandwich courses where you spend part of the time gaining practical experience with an employer). It is also possible to study on a part-time basis with some of these institutions and most notably, of course, with the Open University.

How higher education is catering for the needs of mature students

Credit Accumulation and Transfer (CAT)

Many universities and other HE providers are adopting the CAT system. This includes Assessment of Prior Learning which enables you to obtain recognition for your previous qualifications and learning experiences. It also makes it possible to transfer between courses and between institutions without having to repeat material or levels of study.

Clearly, CAT and APL can facilitate the entry into higher education of older students and those who have had a vocational rather than an academic education.

You can find out who operates CAT and APL by using

ECCTIS 2000 (Education Counselling and Credit Transfer Information Service).

☛ chapter 2 and see the section on computer-based education information systems.

Work-based learning

Many HE providers including universities are now working with local employers to provide learning in the workplace to enable people to update and be accredited for their skills. Such schemes can incorporate CAT and APL as part of the programme.

Find out from your local HE institutions whether they are involved in work-based learning and/or talk to your company's training department about the relevance to your own job.

Finding out who provides what in higher education

There are a number of directories, which should be available in your local careers library, that will tell you what courses are available and where. For example:

The Directory of Higher Education published by CRAC
This publication lists every higher education course available at all universities and colleges in the UK.

Graduate Studies published by CRAC
This title covers all postgraduate courses in the UK, including course synopses of about 120 words each.

Mature students

At the time of writing, there are over 280,000 people aged 25 or over in higher education. Mature students are recognised as being conscientious and successful in their work and as having a lot to offer to the study groups of which they are part. They are welcomed by most universities on this basis. The declining birth rate in the 1970s also means that there are fewer 18 year olds to fill the available places.

Many universities are prepared to waive their usual

entry qualifications for mature students (these are normally at the very least two A-levels or equivalent).

Access courses

If you decide you are not yet ready to tackle studies at degree level, or if your chosen course requires some prior knowledge you haven't got, for example in science, an Access course may be the answer. These are usually provided in FE colleges to prepare people without the usual entry qualifications for degree-level studies. These colleges are normally linked to particular universities which guarantee places to successful Access participants.

Find out from your local FE colleges what they offer in terms of Access courses. If you have a particular university in mind, ask if they have any arrangements with individual FE colleges.

Franchised degrees

Some universities now 'franchise' FE colleges to deliver the first one or two years of their degree courses before students move on to the university for the later part of the course. The advantages for you as a student are that you can continue, for the time being, to study locally in an establishment with which you may already be familiar. You can also expect to work in smaller groups and have more personal contact with your tutor than you would in a university. The downside is that, in general, the library facilities are not as good in FE colleges and you'll miss out on the social life of university. Nevertheless, this arrangement is highly favoured by many students, although provision has not expanded as greatly as was predicted owing to the cuts that have affected HE in general.

Find out from your local FE colleges whether they are involved in franchising arrangements with the HE sector.

Open and distance learning

Open learning is the name given to a system of further

education conducted on a flexible part-time basis. Distance learning is a teaching system consisting of video, audio and written material designed for a person to use in studying a subject at home or in the workplace. Generally, a tutor is available to give advice or mark written work either through correspondence/telephone calls or by occasional meetings.

Open or distance learning are particularly convenient methods of studying and obtaining qualifications in your own time and at your own pace. The learning materials can be excellent and include multi-media packages which can be made up of books, videos, audio cassettes or computer software.

Leading providers, of course, include the Open University. They not only deal in first and postgraduate degree courses but also a range of shorter courses directly related to work. These cover areas such as management, including MBAs, health and social welfare and a programme of scientific updating courses. There are many other providers and some companies are highly committed to using their materials in work-based training.

For further information about open and distance learning courses and the support services that are available, consult the *Open Learning Directory* which should be available in your local careers library. For information about Open University courses, contact:

The Central Enquiry Service
The Open University
PO Box 200
Milton Keynes
Buckinghamshire MK7 6AG
Tel: 01908 653231

Financial help

Financial help is highly important. It is, however, beyond the scope of this book to provide the amount of detail required. Similarly, because of the complexity of the rules and the many exceptions that are made to these, it would be less than helpful to generalise. The major responsibility for public funding of students lies with the local education authorities in England and Wales, Regional or Highland Councils in Scotland and the Education and Library Board in Northern Ireland. There are a number of charities and other organisations in both the private and public sectors that offer financial assistance in various forms to selected groups.

Contact one of the advisory organisations mentioned in chapter 2 and/or the institution in which you want to study. Also, talk to your local education authority (or equivalent). There is a range of relevant literature which will probably be available in their libraries.

The companion volume to this book in the Moving Ahead series, *Coming Back to Education* by Paul Stirner, provides comprehensive information and advice on financial help while studying, including grants, student loans, Access funds, postgraduate awards, Career Development Loans, educational trusts and charities.

Career Development Loans

It is worth mentioning Career Development Loans (CDLs) as they are available to practically any adult who wishes to take full-time, part-time or open learning courses lasting for between one week and a year. They cover up to 80 per cent of course fees, plus books and other course expenses. In some instances CDLs can also be used to cover your living expenses while you do a full-time course.

You can borrow between £300 and £5,000 from the Co-operative, Clydesdale or Barclays Banks. The government pays the interest on the loan during the period of the course and for up to two months afterwards. You subsequently repay the loan along with any further interest.

Tax relief

You may be entitled to a tax rebate against the cost of taking NVQs or SCOTVEC equivalents. Ask your tax office for details. Tax relief is also given to people who themselves pay for training that is directly related to work (where the employer won't pay). The training doesn't have to lead to a qualification and the allowance covers the cost of course fees, essential books, travel and subsistence. You should inform your tax office or accounts department if you think you might qualify.

4 Job-hunting is a Job in Itself

The purpose of this chapter

This chapter shows you how to organise your job hunt by having the right tools and keeping records of your applications. It also shows you how to use personal contacts and make speculative submissions as well as how to identify and approach firms who may have suitable vacancies which they have not advertised. Finally, it suggests ways to review your progress.

It does not include information on writing job applications and CVs or dealing with interviews. There are already large numbers of books on these subjects available in your local bookshop or library. Instead, this book brings together information that is more difficult to locate and is not otherwise available in a single volume.

Organising your job hunt

If you have decided what you have to offer to a prospective employer and what you expect in return, you are now ready to organise your job search and decide where you're going to look for vacancies.

Tools for the job

Getting a job is a job in itself. Like any other job, it pays to be well organised and can be made easier if you have the right tools to hand. You will need the following items.

Stationery

Smart presentation is vital so it's important to use good quality paper for your applications. One of the functions of Jobclubs – in addition to giving support, encouragement and training in the techniques of making job applications – is to provide the material resources such as stamps, stationery, telephones and newspapers.

Word processor/typewriter
Access to a word processor and printer makes it so much easier for you to produce well-presented letters of application and CVs, and then to tailor these to individual vacancies. You can also print multiple copies, all with the same standard of reproduction so you don't need access to a photocopier as you might with a typewriter. If you're not working at present, you could ask the Jobcentre whether they can put you in touch with a college or training organisation which can allow you access to a word processor. You could, if you wish, have your applications prepared by a word-processing bureau or use one of the companies that will produce CVs on your behalf (they advertise regularly in the press).

A typewriter is a much less flexible tool and more difficult to produce good results with if you're not a trained typist. Handwritten applications are not normally acceptable; they are difficult to produce neatly and are often difficult to read. However, some employers will request a handwritten letter of application.

Records
Considerable delays can occur between making an application and receiving a reply or being called for interview. It is important to keep a record of all your applications; don't rely on your memory! If you are tailoring your applications to fit specific jobs it is important to keep a copy of exactly what you have said so you can check this before you attend any interviews.

On the next page are some examples of the sorts of records you might find useful.

For responses to advertisements

Date reply sent	Where and when advertised	Ref. no.	Job title	Company	Date reply from advertiser	Comments

For approaches to people you know

Person to contact	Date contact made and how	Follow-up date	Result	Date next contact to be made	Comments

For approaches to agencies

Agency	Name and tel. no. of agent	Date and method	Result	Date next contact to be made	Comments

Job-hunting can take up a lot of time. If you are unemployed, your efforts are likely to be even more intensive. It can help to set aside a certain amount of time regularly on particular days of the week – including, for example, the days when you know the kind of job you are looking for is advertised in the press.

Using personal contacts

How many people get jobs through people they know?

Because of the subtle and essentially private way in which these networks operate it is difficult to say just how many people secure their jobs in this way. The results of a government survey in 1992 suggest that five per cent of jobs at technician level and above were filled using personal contacts, along with seven per cent of all other jobs. This may be an underestimate as, whilst larger companies tend to use more objective selection procedures, the old-boy network is still a potent force in many areas of work. It's worth seeing what it can do for you.

Whom should you approach?

Jot down the names of all the people whom you think might have any influence in the job market. Then make a note of what you think they might be able to do to help. For example, if after being at home with your family you want to return to work as a fashion designer, you might want to contact your former colleague who is now the head buyer for a large retail outlet and in regular contact with clothing manufacturers.

How should you approach people you know?

Your approach to people you know depends on what they are like and how well you know them. If your relationship is a formal one, for example, a high-ranking boss in your former company or a professor at your old university, then the best approach, following a phone call to solicit their help, might be to send a copy of your CV with a covering note setting out what kind of job you are looking for and any special requirements you have (location, salary, etc). Then confirm how you are going to review your progress. For example, you might agree to contact them in two or three weeks' time. Otherwise, they won't know whether to continue mentioning your name to colleagues or sending you internal job notices, etc.

If your relationship is more personal, then a meeting for lunch or a drink in the early evening might be more appropriate. Even among friends, take care to prepare properly, give them a copy of your CV, let them know exactly what you are looking for, and agree a specific programme for following up progress.

If you are still in employment, make sure you are confident that the people you approach will not compromise your position with your present employer; try to foresee potential conflicts of interest. You may feel sensitive if you are currently unemployed and may not want to discuss this with people you know. Try to overcome your feelings; otherwise you may miss out on a valuable job opportunity. The importance of networking cannot be overemphasised; do not fail to exploit any contact you may have, however tenuous.

Making speculative approaches

An effective way of finding jobs

A government-funded survey of employers' recruitment practices in 1992 showed that – taking occupations as a whole – a greater number of people obtained jobs through making speculative approaches to firms than by any other single means. Thirteen per cent of posts at technician, professional and management level and 18 per cent of all other types of jobs were obtained in this way.

This surprisingly high success rate is explained in part by the fact that employers see speculative approaches as a speedy and cost-effective way of recruiting good quality applicants. As well as making immediate appointments, firms are able to build up waiting lists from which they can quickly fill any subsequent vacancies.

It is also explained by the fact that some firms do not

have a formal recruitment system. Notice of vacancies percolates through the informal network. This seems to work quite well in areas like the media where the number of people wanting to get in always exceeds the number of opportunities.

How to make speculative approaches
Having decided whom you want to contact, ring the company to find out the name of the person who would deal with your application. If you are given the opportunity to speak to them direct you should normally do so. This could help you to prepare the ground for a subsequent written application or, if you're really lucky, lead directly to an interview.

The next step is to send your CV and covering letter stating why you want to work for that particular organisation. A good ploy is to state in your letter that you will ring the recipient on a specific date to follow up the application. This shows some initiative on your part and is more likely to result in a response – if only to forestall your call!

Identifying potential employers

You can identify employers who may have suitable vacancies in a number of ways.

National newspapers
All the broadsheets and some of the tabloids now carry separate business news supplements. From these and the general news sections in the national daily and Sunday papers it is possible to see, for example, which firms are expanding or opening up new branches and therefore most likely to be recruiting additional staff. You can also deduce from existing job advertisements what a company's future requirements are likely to be. For example, if a company is advertising for a new sales manager, there

is every possibility that the appointee will want to inject new blood into the sales team.

Local newspapers

As well as including actual vacancies, local paid and free newspapers will tell you what is happening in business and industry in your local area and which firms are expanding or moving in for the first time. It is also worth obtaining the local newspapers from any other areas where you particularly want to work.

Trade and professional journals

You can expect trade and professional journals to be especially knowledgable about developments in your own particular profession or industry.

Radio and television

Television and both national and local radio provide information about commercial and industrial developments through their news programmes, documentaries and series like *The Money Programme*. They also broadcast programmes specifically concerned with employment and related issues.

Directories and other information about companies

Some of the directories listed on the next page will enable you to locate additional targets for speculative applications; others, such as the Register of Companies, have been included to help you to check up on any companies that you have already identified. Public provision of these directories is being impeded by a lack of cash. It might be easiest to ask your public library where you can obtain the directories and other information about companies to whom you might wish to apply for jobs. Public libraries often have links with other providers, including the university libraries.

Guide to Key British Enterprises published by Dun and Bradstreet
Includes information on turnover and capital, range of activities, trade names, trading styles, company size and names and functions of directors and top personnel.

Kelly's Business Directory published by Kelly's Directories
Provides information on companies based in the UK.

The Municipal Yearbook and Public Services Directory published by Municipal Publications
This annual publication gives comprehensive details of every organisation within the public sector.

Register of Companies
Copies of the latest accounts, balance sheets, names of directors and other financial information can be obtained from the following addresses. A search fee is payable.

Registrar of Companies and Limited Partnerships
Companies House
Crown Way
Maindy
Cardiff CF4 3UZ
Tel: 01222 388588

Companies House
55–71 City Road
London EC1Y 1BB
Tel: 0171-253 9393

Stock Exchange Yearbook published by Macmillan
Provides a brief financial description of all public companies quoted on the Stock Exchange.

UK Kompass Register published by Kompass Publishers
This is published annually in two volumes. One lists companies and includes basic facts about location, activities, directors, staffing; the other is an index of products and

services, cross-referenced to the supplying companies. Seven regional volumes are also available.

Who Owns Whom published by Dun and Bradstreet
This shows the relationship between companies. It is likely to be essential reading if you are currently working for a multiple organisation and want to ensure that you do not approach related companies.

Annual reports
These are produced by public companies and are normally obtainable from their public relations departments. The information is often detailed and likely to be most relevant if you are applying for work at management or professional level.

Extel
This system provides information on CD-ROM on quoted and unquoted companies giving details of financial performance and other data. It is available in some public and academic libraries.

Using the business information services
Private sector business information services are on the increase. If you want to find out where business information services are situated and what they provide, there are a number of relevant directories. Your local public library might be able to help with these too. They include:

Business Information Basics published annually by Headland Press

Directory of Information Services in the UK published by ASLIB

World Directory of Business Information Libraries published by Euromonitor

Reviewing your job-hunting programme

It is important to review your job-hunting programme at regular intervals. Consider again some of the questions you asked yourself when you first thought about setting out on the next stage of your career.

1. How long have I actively been looking for work?

2. What methods am I using to identify suitable vacancies?

    - Personal contacts
    - Speculative submissions
    - National newspapers
    - Local press
    - Trade and professional journals
    - Radio and television
    - Employment/company directories
    - Private agencies
    - Jobcentre

    Are there any I have missed? (Check the lists in the introduction to Part 2.)

    Do the results suggest that I am concentrating on using the right methods? If not, where should my energies be directed?

3. What types of job am I looking for?

4. How many applications have I made so far?

5. How many of these have led to interviews?

6. How many jobs have I been offered and why did I not accept them? With hindsight would I now accept any of these? What does this tell me about how my attitudes have changed?

7. At what stage do I tend to fail?

    ❏ At the short-list stage

    You need to ask:

    ▶ Did I do my homework on the company thoroughly enough?
    ▶ Did my application do me justice and fully reflect the needs of the job?

    ❏ At the interview stage

    You have to decide:

    ▶ Was there a weakness in the way I presented myself?
    ▶ Did I go sufficiently well prepared?
    ▶ Was my attitude unacceptable in any way? Was I too arrogant/unassertive/aggressive/imprecise?

    Look at the literature available on interviewing techniques and, if you are unemployed, consider the help offered through the Jobcentre as described in chapter 6. Do you need to think again about your job requirements?

8. To what extent do my qualifications and experience match up to the jobs available?

9. What other types of job could I consider?

    List them and then decide, using the Introduction to Part 2, how you would go about looking for vacancies.

10. What must I do to update my skills in order to do these jobs? What updating would I need? How could I do this through training?

    ☞ chapter 2 about getting advice on choosing jobs and training; chapter 3 on using the vocational education and training system.

11. Do I need to consider changing my career? How can I get advice about this?

    ☞ chapter 2 for details of the advisory agencies.

12. What salary am I expecting? What is my minimum negotiating figure? Is this realistic?

13. Where could I work without relocating?

14. Would I be prepared to relocate and, if so, where would I be prepared to move to?

15. Have I considered the various forms of self-employment?

    ☞ chapter 5 on alternative ways of working.

16. Should I be thinking of re-working my job application in the light of my job-hunting experience?

5 Alternative Ways of Working

The purpose of this chapter

This chapter explains why more people are becoming self-employed and helps you to consider whether you might set up your own business, operate a franchise, work in a co-operative or take part-time employment or a job-share. It describes some of the services that are available to help you to make this decision and to offer support once you have started in business.

Reasons for the growth in self-employment

The last 20 years or so have brought about dramatic changes in the nature of employment in this country, creating what is now variously referred to as a 'service' economy, 'information' or 'post-industrial' society. These changes have also fundamentally affected the way we work. More people are now self-employed and, with the aid of computers, word processors and fax machines, have been able to set up businesses in their own homes.

Why firms prefer to employ freelancers

About one in seven of those in paid employment in Britain now work for themselves. Increasing numbers of organisations choose to contract freelance workers (or consultants) to do specialised work – such as computer systems analysis – or to provide ancillary services – such as security or cleaning.

The reason for this change is largely financial. By employing freelancers, consultants or contractors, firms are able to pull in these services when they need them and thus avoid the cost of maintaining a pool of labour that could at times be underused. Central government, for instance, now spends about £500 million a year on consultancy services. It is also currently involved in 'market testing', i.e., inviting the private sector to tender for a wide range of services currently provided by civil servants. The second advantage for employers is the reduction in overheads – freelance book-keepers, for example, do not require desk space or a personal computer. The advantage to freelancers is that they are generally paid at a higher rate than if they were direct employees of the organisation. This may or may not be eroded in time spent unproductively, such as travelling. Furthermore, freelancers do not enjoy the benefits of employed staff. Clearly, however, this trend leads to fewer vacancies for directly employed workers.

Would self-employment suit me?

It is worthwhile considering whether self-employment would be a viable option for you – particularly if you do the sort of work that companies are now beginning to sub-contract.

Going into business is a major step for anyone. You will need to do a lot of self-examination and research before deciding to take the plunge. Fortunately, you don't have to make this decision in isolation. There are now a number of organisations which can provide you with professional advice and training, along with dozens of books on the subject. Details of some of these organisations are given later in this chapter.

What do I have to offer?
The first question to ask is what sort of product or service would you offer if you became self-employed. This might be something directly related to your present or last job. On the other hand you might want to pick up on the experience you gained from an earlier employer. This may have been something you particularly enjoyed and

were good at but which no employer has been able to offer you since. Alternatively you may want to make use of skills or knowledge that you have acquired through your leisure activities.

Is my product or service marketable?
You will need to know whether your product is saleable; evaluate your current network of contacts in terms of the amount of work they are likely to bring you; and decide what you are going to do to generate further custom.

Can I go it alone or do I need partners?
Is it possible for one person alone to produce my proposed product or service or do I need to involve others? Do I know anyone who might be interested in joining me in partnership?

Have I got the temperament to go into business on my own?
This covers a whole range of questions such as:

- Would I enjoy going out and finding customers?
- Do I enjoy working on my own?
- Can I make my own decisions? Would I get satisfaction from that?
- Am I adaptable and can I cope with all the uncertainties involved in self-employment?

Will self-employment suit my lifestyle?

- Do I have financial commitments that might be difficult to meet whilst I am getting my business off the ground?
- Will running a business fit in with my family responsibilities? Will my family be supportive or help in the business?
- Am I prepared to let my leisure interests slip in favour of work or are these other interests equally or more important to me?
- Can I travel if the work demands it?

What are the pros and cons of self-employment compared with working for an organisation?

A lot of small firms go bankrupt but a lot of people are made redundant from larger firms too. So the 'security gap' between working for yourself or for someone else has narrowed. Perhaps one of the main contrasts at present is that if you are made redundant by an employer you will probably get a cash settlement. If you go bankrupt you could lose everything. However, severance payments may not stay the norm and there are ways of safeguarding your personal capital if your business goes bust. Similarly, whilst long hours have always been regarded as an essential feature of running one's own business, it is now quite usual for managers in both private organisations and government service to put in extremely long days as posts are cut but overall workloads remain the same. The biggest difference is probably that if you don't work, you don't earn. You will notice the loss of perhaps previously unappreciated benefits such as holiday pay. You will probably need to take out a private pension plan and, perhaps, health insurance.

Another important consideration is whether you have space at home to set up your own business or whether you will have to hire premises. If you have received severance pay, this could help you with your start-up costs and cash-flow while your business is developing. Otherwise, you will have to seek other sources of finance. Working from home is obviously cheaper but means it's harder to draw the line between work and home life. It's very tempting to slip upstairs and do a little more! If you are spending long hours alone each day, you can begin to feel lonely. It's a good idea to draw up a list of the advantages and disadvantages of working for yourself.

To compare being employed with working for yourself you will need to ask questions like:

- ▶ Would I welcome the freedom to be my own boss?
- ▶ Would I prefer to move up the corporate ladder step by step?
- ▶ Do I regard my work as the means to enable me to enjoy my other interests?
- ▶ Will I be happy to stay in paid employment even if there is little prospect of advancement?

Here is a case-study of one man in his early thirties who recently took the decision to become self-employed.

Symbiosis

Symbiosis is a small company of five people which specialises in providing a marketing service to businesses.

'Moving from being employed to self-employed is quite a shock to the system – it is rather like leaving home for the first time. You have total control over what you can do but the limiting factor, as always, is money. Doing the job that you are good at or have been trained to do is the easy bit. It is all the other disciplines associated with running your own business that are hard – selling, marketing, tax returns, VAT and, of course, invoicing and financing work in progress. In my previous job I was a designer working in a large practice. I had not been exposed to the full breadth of these tasks. As a result, I had a massive learning curve to conquer when we started the business. We were very busy doing paying work as well as setting up the company which made it necessary to work long hours – even working all night on many occasions!

The effect on your personal life is drastic – long and irregular hours can put a strain on relationships which in turn can affect your work. My feeling is that in the early days of starting a business you need to be very self-disciplined and focused – almost to the exclusion of everything else. In short, you must be selfish with your time. Fortunately my wife also has a demanding job, so she understands the necessity of being flexible. We both see Symbiosis as a long-term investment – if we believed that it was not going to be a success we would have to re-evaluate the commitment. Making sure that we all have a decent holiday at least once a year allows us to take a complete rest from the intensity of working so hard.

I took a major pay cut when we started Symbiosis. I think if any of us had any serious financial commitments to carry on our own, such as mortgages or families, it would have been too difficult to make ends meet. Especially for the first few years, finding anyone who will give you a mortgage or personal finance is unlikely. There are enough worries associated with running a business without having to think about where the next meal is coming from, so over-extending yourself is not to be recommended. In terms of managing the money within the business, we found it difficult to find anyone who could give us sound financial advice. We have had to learn by our mistakes.

By the end of the second year of trading we have managed to triple our turnover, but we are very aware that we must not grow too quickly as most businesses that fail do so around their second year of trading. Our plans over the next couple of years are: to maintain a steady rate of growth, to invest in order to make us more efficient and to develop our customer base. This will hopefully lead us towards financial stability and enable us to take some money out of the business as well as allowing us to concentrate on what we are good at.

Being self-employed is by its very nature exciting; success or failure is driven by your own self-motivation, confidence and ability to seek market opportunities and exploit them. Having your own business changes your outlook on life in many ways – the level of job satisfaction and interest is greater due to being exposed to a wider range of activities. If there are elements of the job that you do not enjoy, you have the ability to change those aspects or policies with greater ease than if you are in employment. Most of all, I enjoy not feeling guilty about taking a long lunch break or having the occasional late start!

Agencies to help you to decide

The pitfalls and high failure rates of small businesses have been well-publicised. You do, however, have access to a wide range of agencies that can offer you training and counselling before you decide to take the plunge. In many instances these services are free of charge and, in the case of TEC provision, you may qualify for a government training allowance.

You should check with the tax office about self-employment. The Inland Revenue may deny you self-employed status if, for example, you are doing work for one company only. The rules are complicated and it will be worth checking up with your local tax office before you start. Ask your tax office for a copy of the Inland Revenue leaflet IR56/NI39, *Employed or Self-employed?: a guide for tax and national insurance.*

Financial help, advice and training

This guide lists only the main sources of help that are readily available throughout the country.

TECs and LECs

In England and Wales, the Training and Enterprise Councils (TECs) and, in Scotland, Local Enterprise Companies (LECs) administer the government-funded business start-up scheme (formerly known as the Enterprise Allowance Scheme). If you are unemployed and fulfil the other eligibility criteria, they have the discretion to offer you between £20 and £90 per week during the first 26–66 weeks of your new business operation. To be accepted for the scheme, you will need to present a viable business plan. This is a detailed plan setting out the objectives of the business, the strategy and tactics planned to achieve them, and the expected profits, usually over a period of three to ten years. You must also be setting up a new business rather than taking over an existing operation. Your continuing eligibility during this period may be subject to satisfactory reviews carried out by the TEC/LEC. There is, however, no mandatory obligation on TECs or LECs to use their money in this way, so some may drop this scheme in favour of other ways of helping people to start new businesses.

Financial support

As an example, Sheffield TEC's version of the former Enterprise Allowance Scheme is called Build Your Own Business Financial Support. Participants are paid £40 during each of the first 24 weeks of their business operation; then £35 for each of the next 16 weeks; £30 for each of the next 12; then, after an eight-week gap, £50 for each of the next four weeks – in other words, a total of £2,080 over the first 64 weeks of operation.

Training and counselling

TECs and LECs also provide training and counselling in setting up in business, leading to the completion of your business plan. (Your credibility with loan institutions and other business professionals – as well as acceptance for TEC funding – will be directly linked to the quality of that document.) This help is available, free of charge, irrespective of whether you are currently working or unemployed. If you are out of work, you may be eligible for a government training allowance during the training period. If you are working you can take the course in the evening.

Delivery of these training services varies from area to area. With Sheffield TEC's Business Enterprise Programme, for instance, I attended an introductory day followed by six full-day training sessions over six weeks. The time was divided equally between marketing skills, slanted towards establishing a local customer base (relevant, say, to starting a small retail business), and financial management, which would be appropriate to any type of small business. Marketing was taught by an experienced local businessman and finance by a professional accountant; they took you step-by-step through the completion of your business plan in their respective disciplines.

Business counselling was subsequently available on one day per week over each of the next six weeks or until such time as my business plan had been satisfactorily completed and approved by the two tutors. I was then required to attend a fairly searching interview with a business counsellor at the TEC. He explained that the TEC was committed to ensuring that participants had a viable business proposition.

Further free training when you become self-employed
When I had completed the Business Enterprise Programme with Sheffield TEC I was invited to attend a number of other short business courses including bookkeeping, time management, self-presentation and marketing. These were available to anyone who had been in business for less than two years.

Further information about eligibility for financial support and details of their training and counselling services can be obtained by contacting your local TEC or LEC. Their addresses and telephone numbers are set out by region in the annex at the end of this chapter.

Local enterprise agencies/trusts

The other main network of support, which also covers Northern Ireland, is provided by over 400 independent, privately run local enterprise agencies, including 46 enterprise trusts in Scotland. They provide free advice on finance, premises, marketing and other subjects and may be able to help with access to loans, managed workspaces and information services.

For further information about local enterprise agencies/trusts in England and Wales, contact:

Economic Development Division
Business in the Community (BiC)
8 Stratton Street
London W1X 5DF
Tel: 0171-629 1600
Fax: 0171-629 1834

In Scotland, contact:

Scottish Business in the Community (SBC)
Romano House
43 Station Road
Costorphine
Edinburgh EH12 7AF
Tel: 0131-334 9876
Fax: 0131-316 4521

In Northern Ireland, contact:

The Local Enterprise Development Agency
LEDU House
Upper Gallwally
Belfast BT8 4TB
Tel: 01232 419031
Fax: 01232 691432

Local authorities

In addition, many local authorities provide important services to businesses in their area, including advice and information, training, premises and help in raising capital. Your local council offices or library should be able to tell you about these.

For example, Sheffield City Council Development Office, in conjunction with the Sheffield Enterprise Agency and Midland Bank, offers advice and loans of up to £50,000 for viable business propositions, at favourable interest rates, and guarantees the repayment of up to 50 per cent of these loans to the bank. They also provide modern workshop accommodation at 75 per cent discount in the first quarter, 50 per cent in the second and 25 per cent in the third.

The Prince's Youth Business Trusts

These trusts provide specialist business counselling and help to people up to the age of 25 who want to become self-employed. They also give grants and low interest loans to young people who are not otherwise able to raise the necessary money to start a business. They are particularly concerned to develop the talents of disadvantaged young people and to encourage them to help others in the community. For further information, contact:

The Prince's Youth Business Trust
5th Floor
5 Cleveland Place
London SW1 6JJ
Tel: 0171-321 6500

The Prince's Scottish Youth Business Trust
Mercantile Chambers
53 Bothwell Street
Glasgow G2 6TA
Tel: 0141-248 4999

The banks

The relationships between banks and small businesses have been well publicised and you can keep abreast of current developments through the media. However, bank managers have a certain autonomy and how you are treated can vary from branch to branch. Interest rates are variable and, as a new starter, you may be offered concessions like free banking for the first year. Whether, as a new business, you would be in a position to bargain is a subject of debate amongst business counsellors but it may be worth shopping around. As well as being money-lenders, banks are another important source of advice and information about going into business and about the financial viability of your particular plan.

Books and other information

There is a wide range of guides available about self-employment including information about other sources of help and training. The quality of this information varies and it might be worth looking at some of these publications in your local library before you decide to buy.

A good start might be to send for a free information pack entitled *Be Your Own Boss* which is available from:

Federation of Small Businesses
140 Lower Marsh
Westminster Bridge
London SE1 7AE
Tel: 0171-928 9272

Franchising

Franchising is a form of self-employment that is becoming an increasingly popular way for companies to spread their risk and costs – and generate motivation. For example, most milk roundsmen who formerly worked as employees of the dairy now operate on this basis.

Franchising usually involves you in providing goods or services according to a formula devised by the franchisers. You pay them in return for the use of that formula, and possibly the supply of the related goods and equipment and support services – such as training and what can be powerful central advertising (think of Benetton). The required investment is likely to be at least £5,000 and £25,000 is more typical. Once again, the banks should be able to advise on the financial viability.

Many of the best-known franchising companies are involved in retailing, like Benetton (clothing), or fast-food sales, like Burger King or Pizza Express. Dale Farm now franchises its milk rounds; Prontoprint provides a photocopying service and produces personalised stationery and business cards; Dyno-rod provides a drain-cleaning service. For further information, contact:

The British Franchising Association
Thames View
New Town Road
Henley-on-Thames
Oxfordshire RG9 1HG
Tel: 01491 578049

Co-operatives

Worker co-operatives involve groups of people working together and having an equal say in how their businesses operate. They therefore tend to be less solitary than other forms of self-employment. However, the level of commitment and personal qualities required are very similar; many co-operatives show no outward signs of being any different from other commercial enterprises. The stronger entrepreneurial spirit may, however, be frustrated by the consensus decision-making process and reduced potential for high personal financial reward.

Examples of successful co-operatives in Great Britain include credit unions, housing and agriculture but there is virtually no limit to the sort of goods or service that can be delivered by this type of business. There has recently been a marked increase in the number of co-operatives set up by employees of existing companies or people made redundant – often appropriately referred to as 'phoenix' co-operatives. Information about setting up and running this form of business can be obtained from:

Industrial Common Ownership Movement (ICOM)
Vassalli House
20 Central Road
Leeds LS1 6DE
Tel: 01532 461738
Fax: 01532 440002

Scottish Co-operative Development Co Ltd
Building 1
Templeton Street
Bridgeton
Glasgow G40 1DE
Tel: 0141-554 3797
Fax: 0141-554 5163

Northern Ireland Co-operative Development Agency
136 University Street
Belfast BT7 1HH
Tel: 01232 232755

Part-time working

Part-time working has obvious advantages and one obvious drawback: you earn less money. Furthermore, although the law is in the process of change, part-time workers have traditionally had less employment protection, for example, in cases of unfair dismissal and maternity leave. Since the vast proportion of new jobs are part-time, almost half of Britain's workforce is now in part-time employment. For some people, part-time work complements family or other commitments. It can also help from a career point of view by releasing time for further studies. However, for some people there is no other option but to take on two or more part-time jobs.

Job-sharing

You may be interested in doing work that is normally done by one full-time worker but can only fit in part-time working with your other commitments. In this case job-sharing may be the answer. This means that you are paid your salary and are entitled to fringe benefits on a pro-rata basis. Many managers, especially in the public sector, are happy for skilled members of staff to job-share. Employers sense a greater commitment in those who are being given the opportunity to use their experience and take responsibility for their work. Some employers may fear lack of continuity or greater work-related costs but, in practice, job-sharers have shown that they are committed to making job-sharing work. For further information, contact:

New Ways to Work
309 Upper Street
London N1 2TY
Tel: 0171-226 4026

Annex 2: Names and Addresses of TECs and LECs

TECs in England and Wales and LECs in Scotland are listed below in alphabetical order within their region.

England and Wales

South-east

Hampshire TEC
25 Thackery Mall
Fareham
Hampshire PO16 0PQ
Tel: 01329 230099

Heart of England TEC
26–27 The Quadrant
Abingdon Science Park
Barton Lane
Abingdon
Oxfordshire OX14 3YS
Tel: 01235 553249

Isle of Wight Training and
   Enterprise
Mill Court
Furrlongs
Newport
Isle of Wight PO30 2AA
Tel: 01983 8222818

Kent TEC
5th Floor
Mountbatten House
28 Military Road
Chatham
Kent ME4 4JE
Tel: 01634 844411

Milton Keynes and North
   Bucks TEC
Old Market Halls
Creed Street
Wolverton
Milton Keynes
Buckinghamshire MK12 5LY
Tel: 01908 222555

Surrey TEC
Technology House
48–54 Goldsworth Road
Woking
Surrey GU21 1LE
Tel: 01483 728190

Sussex TEC
2nd Floor
Electrowatt House
North Street
Horsham
West Sussex RH12 1RS
Tel: 01403 271471

Thames Valley Enterprise
6th Floor, Kings Point
120 Kings Road
Reading
Berkshire RG1 3BZ
Tel: 01734 568156

London

AZTEC
Manorgate House
Kingston-upon-Thames
Surrey KT2 7AL
Tel: 0181-547 3934

CENTEC (Central London)
12 Grosvenor Crescent
London SW1X 7EE
Tel: 0171-411 3500

CILNTEC
City and Inner London North
80 Great Eastern Street
London EC2A 3DP
Tel: 0171-324 2424

London East TEC
Cityside House
40 Alder Street
London E1 1EE
Tel: 0171-377 1866

North London TEC
Dunmayne House
1 Fox Lane
Palmers Green
London N13 4AB
Tel: 0181-447 9422

North West London TEC
Kirkfield House
118–120 Station Road
Harrow
Middlesex HA1 2RL
Tel: 0181-424 8866

SoLoTEC
Lancaster House
7 Elmfield Road
Bromley
Kent BR1 1LT
Tel: 0181-313 9232

South Thames TEC
200 Great Dover Street
London SE1 4YB
Tel: 0171-403 1990

West London TEC
Sovereign Court
15–21 Staines Road
Hounslow
Middlesex TW3 3HA
Tel: 0181-577 1010

Eastern

Bedfordshire TEC
Woburn Court
2 Railton Road
Woburn Road Industrial Estate
Kempston
Bedfordshire MK42 7PN
Tel: 01234 843100

CambsTEC (Central and South Cambridgeshire)
Units 2–3, Trust Court
The Vision Park
Histon
Cambridge CB4 4PW
Tel: 01223 235633

Essex TEC
Redwing House
Hedgerows Business Park
Colchester Road
Chelmsford
Essex CM2 5PB
Tel: 01245 450123

Greater Peterborough TEC
Unit 4, Blenheim Court
Peppercorn Close
Lincoln Road
Peterborough PE1 2DU
Tel: 01733 890808

Hertfordshire TEC
New Barnes Mill
Cottonmill Lane
St Albans
Hertfordshire AL1 2HA
Tel: 01727 852313

Norfolk and Waveney TEC
Partnership House
Unit 10, Norwich Business Park
Whiting Road
Norwich NR4 6DJ
Tel: 01603 763812

Suffolk TEC
2nd Floor, Crown House
Ipswich
Suffolk IP1 3HS
Tel: 01473 218951

South-west

Avon TEC
PO Box 164
St Lawrence House
29–31 Broad Street
Bristol BS99 7HR
Tel: 0117-927 7116

Annex 2: Names and Addresses of TECs and LECs **83**

Training and Enterprise Councils

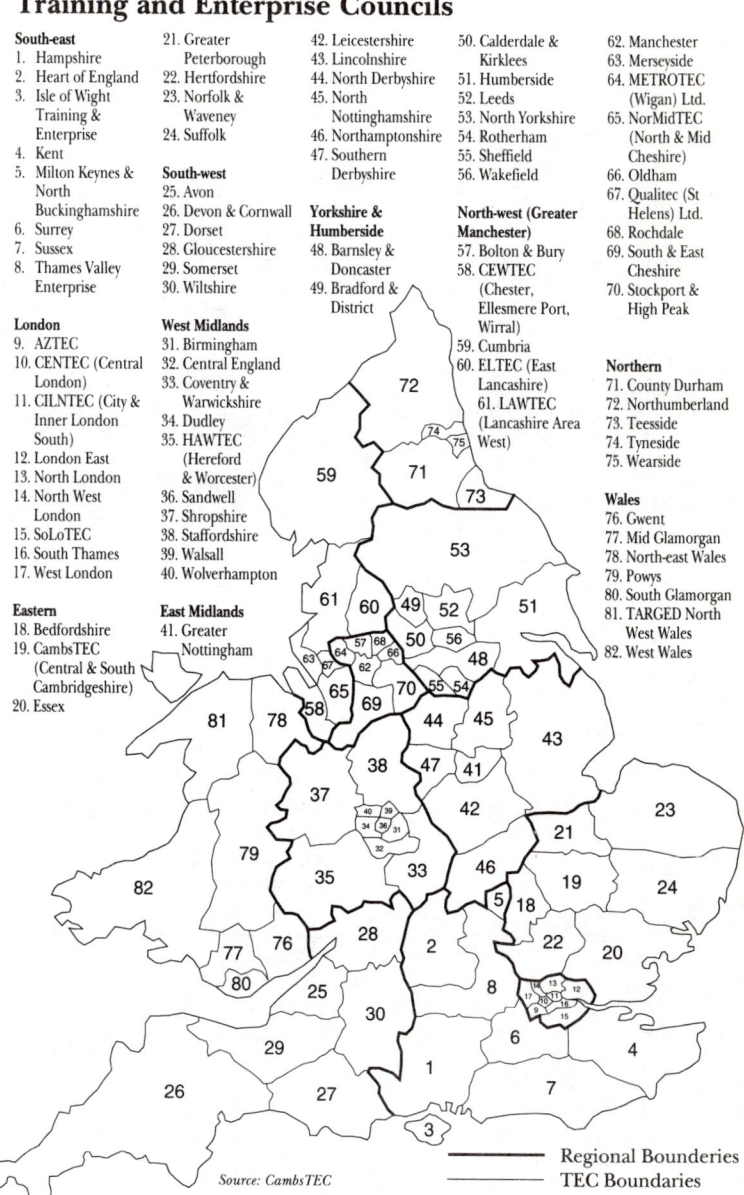

South-east
1. Hampshire
2. Heart of England
3. Isle of Wight Training & Enterprise
4. Kent
5. Milton Keynes & North Buckinghamshire
6. Surrey
7. Sussex
8. Thames Valley Enterprise

London
9. AZTEC
10. CENTEC (Central London)
11. CILNTEC (City & Inner London South)
12. London East
13. North London
14. North West London
15. SoLoTEC
16. South Thames
17. West London

Eastern
18. Bedfordshire
19. CambsTEC (Central & South Cambridgeshire)
20. Essex
21. Greater Peterborough
22. Hertfordshire
23. Norfolk & Waveney
24. Suffolk

South-west
25. Avon
26. Devon & Cornwall
27. Dorset
28. Gloucestershire
29. Somerset
30. Wiltshire

West Midlands
31. Birmingham
32. Central England
33. Coventry & Warwickshire
34. Dudley
35. HAWTEC (Hereford & Worcester)
36. Sandwell
37. Shropshire
38. Staffordshire
39. Walsall
40. Wolverhampton

East Midlands
41. Greater Nottingham
42. Leicestershire
43. Lincolnshire
44. North Derbyshire
45. North Nottinghamshire
46. Northamptonshire
47. Southern Derbyshire

Yorkshire & Humberside
48. Barnsley & Doncaster
49. Bradford & District
50. Calderdale & Kirklees
51. Humberside
52. Leeds
53. North Yorkshire
54. Rotherham
55. Sheffield
56. Wakefield

North-west (Greater Manchester)
57. Bolton & Bury
58. CEWTEC (Chester, Ellesmere Port, Wirral)
59. Cumbria
60. ELTEC (East Lancashire)
61. LAWTEC (Lancashire Area West)
62. Manchester
63. Merseyside
64. METROTEC (Wigan) Ltd.
65. NorMidTEC (North & Mid Cheshire)
66. Oldham
67. Qualitec (St Helens) Ltd.
68. Rochdale
69. South & East Cheshire
70. Stockport & High Peak

Northern
71. County Durham
72. Northumberland
73. Teesside
74. Tyneside
75. Wearside

Wales
76. Gwent
77. Mid Glamorgan
78. North-east Wales
79. Powys
80. South Glamorgan
81. TARGED North West Wales
82. West Wales

Source: CambsTEC

—— Regional Boundaries
—— TEC Boundaries

Devon and Cornwall TEC
Foliot House
Brooklands
Budshead Road
Crownhill
Plymouth
Devon PL6 5XR
Tel: 01752 767929

Dorset TEC
26 Oxford Road
Bournemouth
Dorset BH8 8EY
Tel: 01202 299284

Gloucestershire TEC
Conway House
33–35 Worcester Street
Gloucester GL1 3AJ
Tel: 01452 524488

Somerset TEC
Crescent House
3–7 The Mount
Taunton
Somerset TA1 3TT
Tel: 01823 259121

Wiltshire TEC
The Bora Building
Westlea Campus
Westlea Down
Swindon
Wiltshire SN5 7EZ
Tel: 01793 513644

West Midlands

Birmingham TEC
Chaplin Court
80 Hurst Street
Birmingham B5 4TG
Tel: 0121-622 4419

Central England TEC
The Oakes
Clewes Road
Redditch
Worcestershire B98 7ST
Tel: 01527 545415

Coventry and Warwickshire TEC
Brandon Court
Progress Way
Coventry
West Midlands CV3 2TE
Tel: 01203 635666

Dudley TEC
Dudley Court South
Waterfront East
Level Street
Brierly Hill
West Midlands DY5 1XN
Tel: 01384 485000

HAWTEC (Hereford and Worcester)
Haswell House
St Nicholas Street
Worcester WR1 1UW
Tel: 01905 723200

Sandwell TEC
1st Floor, Kingston House
438–450 High Street
West Bromwich
Sandwell
West Midlands B70 9LD
Tel: 0121-525 4242

Shropshire TEC
2nd Floor, Hazledine House
Central Square
Telford
Shropshire TF3 4JJ
Tel: 01952 291471

Staffordshire TEC
Festival Way
Festival Park
Stoke on Trent
Staffordshire ST1 5TQ
Tel: 01782 291471

Walsall TEC
5th Floor, Townend House
Townend Square
Walsall WS1 1NS
Tel: 01922 32322

Wolverhampton TEC
Pendeford Business Park
Wobaston Road
Wolverhampton WV9 5HA
Tel: 01902 397787

East Midlands

Greater Nottingham TEC
Marina Road
Castle Marina Park
Nottingham NG7 1TN
Tel: 0115-941 3313

Leicestershire TEC
Meridian East
Meridian Business Centre
Leicester LE3 2WZ
Tel: 0116-265 1515

Lincolnshire TEC
5th Floor, Wigford House
Brayford Wharf
Lincoln LN4 7AY
Tel: 01522 532266

North Derbyshire TEC
Block C, St Mary's Court
St Mary's Gate
Chesterfield
Derbyshire S41 7TD
Tel: 01246 551158

North Nottinghamshire TEC
1st Floor, Block C, Edwinstone House
High Street
Edwinstone
Mansfield
Nottinghamshire NG21 9PR
Tel: 01623 824624

Northamptonshire TEC
Royal Pavilion
Summerhouse Road
Moulton Park
Northampton NN3 1WD
Tel: 01604 671200

Southern Derbyshire TEC
St Helen's Court
St Helen's Street
Derby DE1 3GY
Tel: 01332 290550

Yorkshire and Humberside

Barnsley and Doncaster TEC
Conference Centre
Eldon Street
Barnsley
South Yorkshire S70 2JL
Tel: 01226 248088

Bradford and District TEC
Fountain Hall
Fountain Street
Bradford
West Yorkshire BD1 3QL
Tel: 01274 723711

Calderdale and Kirklees TEC Ltd
Parkview House
Woodvale Office Park
Woodvale Road
Brighouse
West Yorkshire HD6 4AB
Tel: 01484 400770

Humberside TEC
The Maltings
Silvester Square
Silvester Street
Hull
North Humberside HU1 3HL
Tel: 01482 226491

Leeds TEC
Belgrave Hall
Belgrave Street
Leeds
West Yorkshire LS2 8DD
Tel: 0113-234 7666

North Yorkshire TEC
TEC House
7 Pioneer Business Park
Amy Johnson Way
Clifton Moorgate
York
North Yorkshire YO3 8TN
Tel: 01904 691939

Rotherham TEC
Moorgate House
Moorgate Road
Rotherham
South Yorkshire S60 2EN
Tel: 01709 830511

Sheffield TEC
St Mary's Court
St Mary's Road
Sheffield
South Yorkshire S2 2QA
Tel: 0114-270 1911

Wakefield TEC
Grove Hall
60 College Grove Road
Wakefield
West Yorkshire WF1 3RN
Tel: 01924 929907

North-west

Bolton and Bury Training and
  Enterprise Council Ltd
Clive House
Clive Street
Bolton
Lancashire BL1 1ET
Tel: 01204 397350

CEWTEC
Woodside Business Park
Birkenhead
Wirral
Merseyside L41 1EH
Tel: 0151-650 0555

Cumbria TEC
Venture House
Regents Court
Guard Street
Workington
Cumbria CA14 4EW
Tel: 01900 66991

ELTEC (East Lancashire)
Red Rose Court
Petre Road
Clayton Business Park
Clayton-le-Moor
Lancashire PR1 1HE
Tel: 01772 200035

LAWTEC (Lancashire Area
  West)
4th Floor, Duchy House
96 Lancaster Road
Preston
Lancashire PR1 1HE
Tel: 01772 200035

Manchester TEC
Boulton House
17–21 Chorlton Street
Manchester M1 3HY
Tel: 0161-236 7222

Merseyside TEC
3rd Floor, Tithebarn House
Tithebarn Street
Liverpool L2 2NZ
Tel: 0151-236 0026

METROTEC (Wigan) Ltd
Buckingham Row
Northway
Wigan
Greater Manchester WN1 1XX
Tel: 01942 36312

NorMidTEC (North and Mid
  Cheshire)
Spencer House
Dewhurst Road
Birchwood
Warrington
Cheshire WA3 7PP
Tel: 01925 826515

Oldham TEC
Meridian Centre
King Street
Oldham
Lancashire OL8 1EZ
Tel: 0161-620 0006

Qualitec (St Helens) Ltd
7 Waterside Court
Technology Campus
St Helens
Merseyside WA9 1UE
Tel: 01744 24433

Rochdale TEC
St James Place
160–162 Yorkshire Street
Rochdale
Lancashire OL16 2DL
Tel: 01706 44909

South and East Cheshire TEC
PO Box 37
Middlewich Industrial Estate &
  Business Park
Dalton Way
Middlewich
Cheshire CW10 0HU
Tel: 01606 737009

Stockport and High Peak TEC
1 St Peters Square
Stockport
Greater Manchester SK1 1NN
Tel: 0161-477 8830

Northern

County Durham TEC
Valley Street North
Darlington
County Durham DL1 1TJ
Tel: 01325 351166

Northumberland TEC
Suite 2, Craster Court
Manor Walk Shopping Centre
Cramlington
Northumberland NE23 6XX
Tel: 01670 713303

Teesside TEC
Training and Enterprise
  House
2 Queens Square
Middlesbrough
Cleveland TS2 1AA
Tel: 01642 231023

Tyneside TEC
Moongate House
5th Avenue Business Park
Team Valley Trading Estate
Gateshead
Tyne and Wear NE38 7ST
Tel: 0191-487 5599

Wearside TEC
Derwent House
New Town Centre
Washington
Tyne and Wear NE38 7ST
Tel: 0191-416 6161

Wales

Gwent TEC
Glyndwr House
Unit B2, Cleppa Park
Newport
Gwent NP9 1YE
Tel: 01633 817777

Mid Glamorgan TEC
Unit 17–20, Centre Court
Main Avenue
Treforest Industrial Estate
Pontypridd
Mid Glamorgan CF37 5YL
Tel: 01443 841594

North East Wales TEC
Wynnstay Block
Hightown Barracks
Kingsmill Road
Wrexham
Clwyd LL13 8BH
Tel: 01978 290049

Powys TEC
1st Floor, St Davids House
Newtown
Powys SY16 1RB
Tel: 01686 622494

South Glamorgan TEC
3–7 Drakes Walk
Waterfront 2000
Atlantic Wharf
Cardiff CF1 5AN
Tel: 01222 451000

TARGED North West Wales
  TEC
Llys Brittania
Parc Menal
Bangor
Gwynedd LL57 4BN
Tel: 01258 671444

West Wales TEC
Orchard House
Orchard Street
Swansea
West Glamorgan SA1 5DJ
Tel: 01792 460355

Scotland

Scottish Enterprise Area

Scottish Enterprise
120 Bothwell Street
Glasgow
Strathclyde G2 7JP
Tel: 0141-248 2700

Dumfries and Galloway
  Enterprise Company
Cairnsmore House
Bankend Road
Dumfries
Dumfries and Galloway
  DG1 4TA
Tel: 01387 54444

Dunbartonshire Enterprise
2nd Floor, Spectrum House
Clydebank Business Park
Clydebank
Glasgow
Strathclyde G81 2DR
Tel: 0141-951 2121

Enterprise Ayrshire Ltd
17–19 Hill Street
Kilmarnock
Strathclyde KA3 1HA
Tel: 01563 26623

Forth Valley Enterprise
Laurel House
Laurelhill Business Park
Stirling
Central FK7 9JQ
Tel: 01786 51919

Glasgow Development Agency
Atrium Court
50 Waterloo Street
Glasgow
Strathclyde G2 6HQ
Tel: 0141-204 1111

Grampian Enterprise Co.
27 Albyn Place
Aberdeen
Grampian AB1 1YL
Tel: 01224 211500

Lanarkshire Development
  Agency
New Lanarkshire House
Willow Drive
Strathclyde Business Park
Bellshill
Strathclyde ML4 3AD
Tel: 01698 745454

Lothian and Edinburgh
  Enterprise Ltd
Apex House
99 Haymarket Terrace
Edinburgh
Lothian EH12 5HD
Tel: 0131-313 4000

Moray, Badenoch & Strathspey
  Enterprise Co Ltd
Elgin Business Centre
Elgin
Grampian IV30 1RH
Tel: 01343 550 567

Renfrewshire Enterprise
25–29 Causeyside Street
Paisley
Strathclyde PA1 1UG
Tel: 0141-848 0101

Scottish Borders Enterprise
Bridge Street
Galashiels
Borders TD1 1SW
Tel: 01896 58991

Scottish Enterprise Fife Ltd
Huntsmans House
33 Cadham Centre
Glenrothes
Fife KY7 6RU
Tel: 01592 621000

Annex 2: Names and Addresses of TECs and LECs **89**

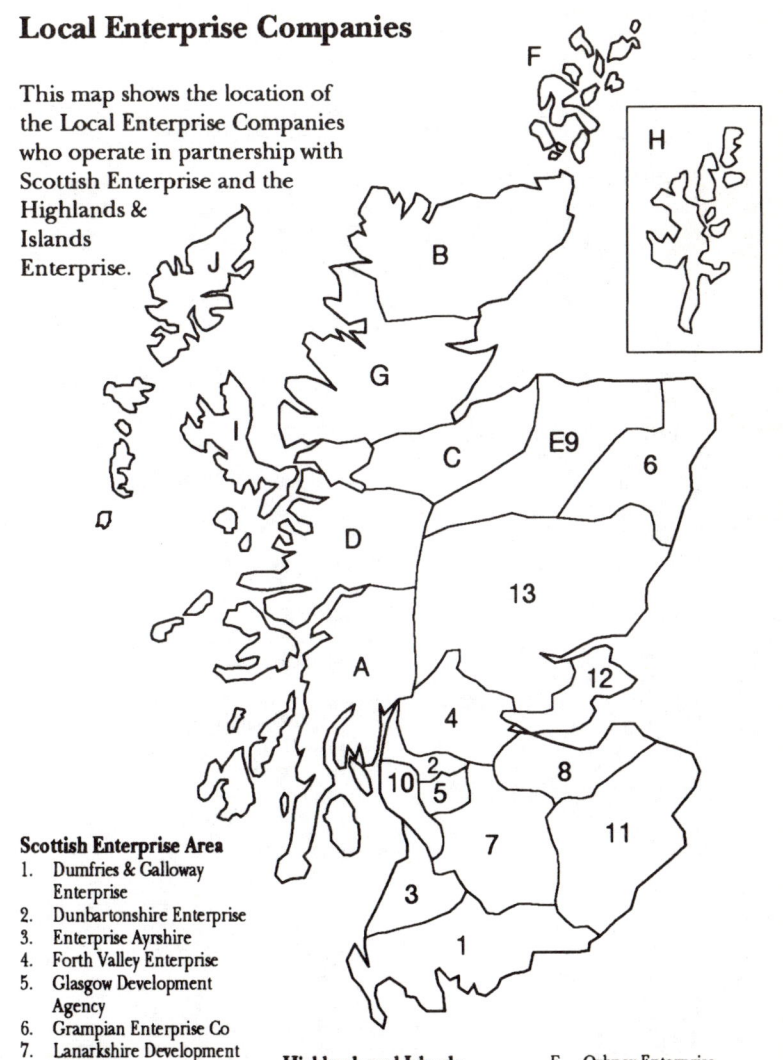

Local Enterprise Companies

This map shows the location of the Local Enterprise Companies who operate in partnership with Scottish Enterprise and the Highlands & Islands Enterprise.

Scottish Enterprise Area
1. Dumfries & Galloway Enterprise
2. Dunbartonshire Enterprise
3. Enterprise Ayrshire
4. Forth Valley Enterprise
5. Glasgow Development Agency
6. Grampian Enterprise Co
7. Lanarkshire Development Agency
8. Lothian & Edinburgh Enterprise Ltd
E9. Moray, Badenoch & Strathspey Enterprise*
10. Renfrewshire Enterprise
11. Scottish Borders Enterprise
12. Scottish Enterprise Fife Ltd
13. Scottish Enterprise Tayside

Highlands and Islands Enterprise Area
A. Argyll & Islands Enterprise
B. Caithness & Sutherland Enterprise
C. Inverness & Nairn Enterprise
D. Lochaber Ltd
E9. Moray, Badenoch and Strathspey Enterprise*
F. Orkney Enterprise
G. Ross & Cromarty Enterprise
H. Shetland Enterprise
I. Skye & Lochalsh Enterprise
J. Western Isles Enterprise

* Operates jointly between Scottish Enterprise and Highlands & Islands Enterprise

Source: Scottish Enterprise Network

Scottish Enterprise Tayside
Enterprise House
45 North Lindsay Street
Dundee
Tayside DD1 1HT
Tel: 01382 23100

Highlands and Islands Enterprise Area

Highlands and Islands
 Enterprise
Bridge House
29 Bridge Street
Inverness
Highland IV1 1QR
Tel: 01463 234171

Argyll and Islands Enterprise
Stag Chambers
Lorne Street
Lochgilphead
Strathclyde PA31 8LU
Tel: 01546 602281

Caithness and Sutherland
 Enterprise
Scape House
Castlegreen Road
Thurso
Highland KW14 7LS
Tel: 01847 66115

Inverness and Nairn
 Enterprise
Castle Wynd
Inverness
Highland IV2 3DW
Tel: 01463 713504

Lochaber Ltd
5 Cameron Square
Fort William
Highland PH33 6AJ
Tel: 01397 704326

Moray, Badenoch and
 Strathspey Enterprise
 Company
Elgin Business Centre
Elgin
Grampian IV30 1RH
Tel: 01343 550 567

Orkney Enterprise
14 Queen Street
Kirkwall
Orkney Islands KW15 1JE
Tel: 01856 874638

Ross and Cromarty Enterprise
62 High Street
Invergordon
Highland IV18 0DH
Tel: 01856 874638

Shetland Enterprise
Toll Clock Shopping Centre
26 North Road
Lerwick
Shetland ZE1 0DE
Tel: 01595 3177

Skye and Lochalsh Enterprise
Kings House
The Green
Portree
Isle of Skye IV51 9BT
Tel: 01478 2841

Western Isles Enterprise
 (Iomairt nan Eilean Siar)
Cromwell Street Quay
Stornoway
Isle of Lewis
Western Isles PA87 2DF
Tel: 01851 703625

2

How Employers Recruit their Staff

Introduction: Where to Find Job Vacancies

This introduction is designed to get you thinking straight away about the wide range of methods that people use to find jobs – and to help you decide which of these are likely to be relevant in your own case. The chapters that follow describe these techniques in detail and explain how you can use them to your best advantage.

The following figures are included for interest but they also show you the importance of some ways of applying for jobs which you might otherwise overlook. For example, it is perhaps surprising that about eight per cent of jobs at technician level and above, and almost 20 per cent of jobs below that level, were obtained through making speculative approaches to employers. (The figures used here come from a government-funded survey carried out in 1992 showing how a sample of 6,000 employers over the country had filled 22,000 vacancies.)

How people get jobs

Eighty per cent of jobs in the following groups:

- routine/unskilled jobs
- operative/assembly work
- sales work
- personal and security services
- skilled craft jobs
- skilled service work
- clerical and secretarial jobs

were obtained by the methods described below:

- 19% by replying to advertisements in paid-for local newspapers
- 18% by making speculative submissions
- 18% by applying through Jobcentres

- ▶ 12% by responding to advertisements in trade and other specialist publications
- ▶ 8% by replying to advertisements on employers' internal notice boards
- ▶ 8% by having been personally recommended, usually by an employee
- ▶ 7% by being taken back on by a former employer (21% of sales staff and a high percentage of building and some manufacturing vacancies were filled in this way)
- ▶ 6% by applying through fee-charging agencies.

The other six methods that led to people getting these types of job were:

- ▶ from waiting lists drawn up from speculative approaches
- ▶ by applying to vacancies notified to the careers service
- ▶ by replying to job advertisements in the local free press
- ▶ by responding to notices on employers' premises facing onto the street
- ▶ by being retained by an employer after originally joining as a YTS trainee or as a participant in another government training programme
- ▶ by recruitment through a trade union or other association.

Jobs in the following occupations:

- ▶ professional
- ▶ professional associate (eg accounting technician)
- ▶ managerial/administration

were mainly obtained by the following methods of application:

- ▶ 30% by responding to job advertisements in professional, trade and other specialist publications

- ▶ 12% through direct applications
- ▶ 12% through the use of fee-charging agencies
- ▶ 10% by responding to internal notices on employers' premises
- ▶ 5% through personal recommendation.

The national press was not covered specifically in this survey although they clearly play a major role in filling jobs at the professional level, often through advertisements placed by recruitment consultants.

6 Jobcentres, Recruitment Agencies and Consultants

The purpose of this chapter

This chapter looks at the different types of employment and recruitment agencies and consultancies and the kind of help you can expect to get from them.

Jobcentres

Jobcentres are run by the government-funded Employment Service and are now generally housed with the unemployment benefit offices. The address of your local centre can be found in the telephone directory under Employment Service. You can ring them to make an appointment if you wish to claim benefit or discuss the other services available – or just call in to look at the jobs, which are all on display.

Jobcentres handle all types of jobs but are stronger on filling manual, personal service (domestic, catering, etc) and security service occupations, followed by sales, clerical and secretarial vacancies.

Jobcentres have a range of free leaflets and booklets on display about job-hunting and related issues and a reference section with publications such as the *Open Learning Directory* and careers literature.

Whilst the vacancy service is open to everyone, the other Jobcentre services are largely designed to help people who are unemployed and have been registered as such for a specified minimum length of time. This time condition is, however, waived in particular cases – including unemployed people with disabilities, ex-offenders, ex-servicemen and women, returners to the labour market and those involved in mass redundancies. It's worth asking if there are any exceptions that would apply to you.

Advisory services

If you sign on for state benefits, you will see a client adviser who will help you to draw up a 'back-to-work plan' and tell you how the Employment Service can help. If you remain unemployed for three months you may then be offered a further interview to discuss your progress and what further help the Employment Service might be able to give you.

Job review workshops

After you have been unemployed for three months you may be eligible for a two-day job review workshop. These are intended to help people from a professional, administrative or executive background who want to explore new career opportunities.

Job search seminars

The three months' unemployment rule normally applies to job search seminars too. These take place over four days, spread over five weeks, and are designed to help you improve your job-hunting and interviewing techniques. Resources – like a telephone, stationery and stamps – are freely available to make job applications.

Travel to interview scheme

In the meantime, after you have been registered as unemployed for more than four weeks, the Jobcentre may pay the cost of your travel and overnight stay to attend interviews in other parts of the UK.

Jobclubs

These are a well-proven way of helping people get back into employment. All the facilities required to make job applications are provided, including stationery, stamps, telephones and newspapers, along with the guidance of a Jobclub leader. You normally have to be unemployed for six months to be eligible.

The Restart Programme
If you remain unemployed for six months you are offered another interview with an adviser. It is at this stage that you would normally become eligible for a place on a Training for Work course or in a Jobclub.

Jobplan workshops
Jobplan workshops are to help people who have been unemployed for 12 months or more decide where their aptitudes lie and what they want to do in the future. They run for a total of five days.

Other schemes for unemployed people
In addition, the Jobcentre can offer a range of schemes designed to bring you in contact with a potential employer and enable you to decide whether the two of you are mutually suited. At the time of writing these are variously known as Job Interview Guarantee and, rather confusingly, Work Trial and Employment on Trial. It will be best to ask what is available at the time.

Training for Work
This is the current generic term for the training programme delivered through the Training and Enterprise Councils for unemployed adults. The programme might take the form of job-specific training, work towards a National Vocational Qualification, work preparation, temporary work to keep your skills up to date or a mixture of these options. At the time of writing, participants receive their usual unemployment benefit or income support allowance topped up by £10 per week.

Further information about these and other services is contained in leaflet EMPL 48 which is available from Jobcentres.

Recruitment agencies

The government-funded survey in 1992 of 22,000 appointments showed that fee-charging agencies fill six per cent of jobs overall, 12 per cent of managerial/administrative jobs and nine per cent of clerical/secretarial appointments – with the last group representing by far the largest actual number of appointments made in this way.

Where to find out about these agencies

There are about 15,000 organisations in this country operating an employee recruitment service. As a rule they charge the employer for filling a vacancy rather than the job applicant. Many of them operate under a voluntary code of practice devised by the Association of Search and Selection Consultants.

About 2,500 agencies are members of the Federation of Recruitment and Employment Services; this produces a *Yearbook of Recruitment and Employment Services* which lists these agencies and shows what types of job each covers. They plan to publish a new edition in late 1994. This may be available in your local reference library. For further information, contact:

The Federation of Recruitment and Employment
 Services
36–38 Mortimer Street
London W1N 7RB
Tel: 0171-323 4300
Fax: 0171-255 2879

Another useful reference source is the *CEPEC Recruitment Guide: a directory of recruitment agencies and search consultants in the UK.* This gives information about how these companies operate and describes and includes tips on how to cope with their selection methods. At the time of writing the latest available edition was published in 1991, but a new edition is expected to be ready in July 1995. For further information, contact:

CEPEC Ltd
67 Jermyn Street
London SW14 6NY
Tel: 0171-930 0322

In addition, the *Human Resources Management Yearbook 1993* includes the names and addresses of around 1,500 of what it describes as 'all the significant companies working in the search selection field from executive search to employment bureaux'. This shows which organisations deal with specific occupations, levels of management, particular industries and so on, amounting to 55 categories in all. The *Yearbook* is published by:

AP International Services
33 Ashbourne Avenue
London NW11 0DU

Details of local organisations can be found in *Yellow Pages* under Employment Agencies and Consultants and Personnel Consultants. You will also be able to see which companies deal with your sort of work when they advertise for candidates for specific job vacancies in your newspaper or trade journal.

Employment bureaux

As well as providing a recruitment service, employment bureaux often act as the employer for the people they place in work, particularly in the case of temporary appointments. They include the well-known companies that operate branches in high streets throughout the country and whose addresses can be discovered in *Yellow Pages*. Alfred Marks, for example, will deal with any occupation. Manpower PLC handles both temporary and permanent commercial and industrial vacancies, including word processing, data entry and drivers. Reed Personnel Services PLC deals with permanent and temporary secretarial and office staff, including accountancy, insurance and computing, along with nursing and other jobs in the care professions, plus technical and catering occupations.

Recruitment consultants

Recruitment consultants – also known as search agencies – search for candidates for specific jobs from technician through professional occupations and up to chief executive/director level. They often advertise these jobs in newspapers and trade journals and may use the replies they get to build up a bank of candidates for future jobs. You should therefore tell them if you want to be considered only for the specific advertised vacancy.

You could select appropriate agencies/consultants and send them your CV asking whether they would consider you for relevant vacancies. It is important to tell the agencies of any organisations you would not want them to approach in case this might jeopardise your current job.

Some of these companies deal with specific types of jobs, for example:

Metier Professional Recruitment
9 Roseberry Crescent
Edinburgh EH2 5JP
Tel: 0131-313 2440

Metier specialises in electronics design and manufacture, data processing and engineering, software and mechanical engineering.

There are a particularly large number of agencies dealing with computer vacancies, including:

Computer Help
1 & 2 Ambassador House
Wolseley Road
Harrow
Middlesex HA3 5RY
Tel: 0181-861 6060

Computer Help deals with contract and permanent computer personnel, including consultants, analysts, programmers, operators, data entry clerks, technical support and word processor operators.

Other specialists include:

Judy Farquharson Ltd
47 New Bond Street
London W1Y 9HA
Tel: 0171-493 8824

Judy Farquharson specialises in publishing and media appointments from sales and marketing assistants to commissioning editors.

One agency, at least, is involved in helping people with disabilities to gain and retain employment commensurate with their skills and experience. This is:

The Association of Disabled Professionals
170 Benton Hill
Benton
Horbury
West Yorkshire WF4 5HW
Tel: 01924 270335

Others deal with particular industries or groups of industries, including:

The Davis Company
32–34 Great Titchfield Street
London W1P 7AD
Tel: 0171-323 6696
Fax: 0171-323 6697

The Davis Company handles marketing, advertising, PR, sales promotion, design, media, sales and publishing.

Morgan Cairns Associates Ltd
550 Ley Street
Newberry Park
Ilford
Essex IG2 7DB
Tel: 0181-518 5757

Morgan Cairns Associates specialises in medical and supplementary professions, including doctors, radiographers, dieticians, speech therapists, pharmacists and physiotherapists.

Ashbrittle Limited
Lower Dagnall Street
St Albans
Hertfordshire AL3 4PA
Tel: 017278 54054
Fax: 017278 54054

Ashbrittle Limited operates as international consultants to the construction industry and allied trades.

Others are involved in executive search and selection across the full range of industries; these include one of the largest firms:

Hoggett Bowers Search and Selection
5 London Bridge Street
London SE1 9SG
Tel: 0171-403 7000
Fax: 0171-403 3773

Bradford Training and Enterprise Council has set up the People of Previous Experience (POPE) Agency to help people over 50 *in the Bradford area only* to find employment. This is in response to the concern expressed by government ministers and others about ageist attitudes at work. It is likely that other TECs will follow suit. You will find the address and telephone number of your local TEC in the annex to chapter 5.

POPE Recruitment Services
Phoenix House
Rushton Avenue
Bradford
West Yorkshire BD3 7BH
Tel: 01274 660936

Headhunters

Headhunters will, by definition, contact *you* if through their research they identify you as having the special skills, qualifications and experience to fill a particular opening for one of their clients. They may, however, welcome a direct approach from you if you have good qualifications and are clearly successful in your field of work. In this case, you would need to identify the headhunting firms who deal with your chosen area of work (you could use one of the directories mentioned above) and then send a brief CV sharply focused on your achievements and stating your ambitions and requirements for the future.

7 Using the Media

The purpose of this chapter

This chapter will help you identify quickly where and when particular vacancies and other work-related information appear in the national daily and Sunday press. It also considers how local and regional newspapers can be used as a source of job vacancies, news about employment-related issues and targets for speculative submissions. It shows why trade, professional and other periodicals are an important source of job vacancies and how some carry a much wider range of occupations than you would expect from their titles. Publications dedicated to advertising job vacancies are also included. Finally, it enables you to make use of radio and television as a source of information about job vacancies and related topics, such as vocational education and training and self-employment – as well as targets for speculative job applications.

Finding your way around the national press

As well as advertising job vacancies, the national press provides a great deal of other information which will be useful to you as a job-seeker – employment trends, careers and vocational education and training. It also gives useful clues about potential job opportunities through more general news stories and features on business and economic matters.

Some newspapers specialise in particular types of vacancies and/or feature specific job vacancies – and, in some cases, related features – on particular days of the week. This chapter identifies these patterns.

Vacancies and job-related information in the national dailies

Every national daily and Sunday newspaper that provides any information about jobs is included here but the extent to which each newspaper is covered varies according to how much detail each of them was able and prepared to provide.

Daily Express

The *Daily Express* has a general appointments section on Tuesday which features jobs, including work overseas in a wide range of occupations and countries, and vocational training courses. On Wednesdays and Thursdays it covers similar information under the title of 'Careers Plus'. Occasional features on careers and education tend to appear on Thursdays.

Daily Mail

Job vacancies are advertised on Thursdays in the 'Careers Mail on Thursday' feature, which is part of the main tabloid, along with editorial features. It includes sales, sales management, retailing, secretarial, financial and especially printing and allied trades vacancies.

Daily Mirror

The *Daily Mirror* carries recruitment advertising on Tuesdays with emphasis on construction workers (including vacancies in the Netherlands), security, and retail management trainees. Vacancies tend to be advertised on the basis of the paper's four regional editions. It includes editorials on job-related issues. Vacancies for A-level school-leavers are advertised around April and May.

The Daily Telegraph

The *Daily Telegraph* currently carries around two-thirds of all professional engineering vacancies (civil, mechanical and production) advertised in the 'quality' press. It is also the market leader on senior management appointments (salaries of £37,500 plus) and is strong on sales representatives, sales and marketing management, finance, accountancy, computer, secretarial and other commercial appointments.

It carries job advertisements from Monday to Saturday and includes a separate supplement on Thursdays entitled 'Telegraph Appointments'. This is repeated with the *Sunday Telegraph* City and Business section. Specialist sections are also published on Tuesdays on general engineering, sales and marketing and other appointments; and on Saturdays, featuring executive positions with salaries over £30,000.

The Financial Times
The *Financial Times* carries vacancies on Wednesdays in banking and City jobs and on Thursdays in accountancy. It is also the definitive source, amongst newspapers in Great Britain, for news on all business and financial issues.

The Guardian
At the time of writing, the *Guardian* is the overall market leader in recruitment advertising. Surveys show that in November 1993 it carried over 40 per cent of the jobs advertised during that month in the 'quality' press and over 47 per cent of all advertised graduate vacancies. It currently dominates the market in creative and media, health, public sector, social services and 'environmental' appointments and leads in science and technology.

Job advertisements appear, along with features about courses and other related topics, in *Guardian 2*, which is published daily in tabloid form as a supplement to the main broadsheet. Specialist categories of vacancies appear on particular days of the week, as follows:
Monday: creative, media and marketing appointments (85 per cent of all the creative and media vacancies advertised in the 'quality' press) and secretarial appointments.

Tuesday: higher education and primary and secondary school appointments (and, during term-time, articles for teachers on practice in schools, particularly on translating the National Curriculum into coursework; details of professional courses for teachers). Also, international appointments (☞ chapter 8 for the section on overseas vacancies advertised in national newspapers).

Wednesday: health service appointments (along with extensive editorial coverage of health matters); other public sector appointments including social services and community care; personnel and training; probation and prison services; senior appointments; health; legal and finance.

Thursday: computer, science and technology and commercial appointments other than in the media. Also includes editorial related to computing issues and careers features for students and graduates.

Friday: housing, conservation, planning and leisure appointments.

Saturday: features a pull-out 'Careers Guardian' which includes a repeat of the commercial vacancies that have been advertised on Monday and Thursday.

The Independent

As befits the youngest of the 'qualities', the *Independent* is the fastest-growing newspaper in terms of recruitment advertising, showing a year-on-year increase of 29 per cent. The daily pattern of job advertisements is as follows:

Monday: computer, engineering, science and technology appointments.

Tuesday: financial, accountancy and European business appointments.

Wednesday: media, marketing and sales.

Thursday: public, education, charity, graduate and general appointments.

Friday: legal.

Morning Star
The *Morning Star* carries occasional advertisements for trades union appointments.

The Sun
The *Sun* advertises job vacancies on Tuesdays and Thursdays and job-related courses mainly on Thursdays. It covers a range of jobs including sales, catering, engineering, paint spraying and vacancies abroad in the construction industry.

The Times
The pattern of job advertising in *The Times* is as follows:
Monday: educational appointments.
Tuesday: computing, secretarial and clerical.
Wednesday: media, arts and secretarial.
Thursday: professional, top management, accounts and finance, sales, marketing, science, engineering and technology.
Friday: computing and information technology.

Today
The pattern of job advertisements in *Today* is exactly the same as in the *Sun*.

The national Sunday newspapers

The Independent on Sunday
This includes general appointments and a business supplement.

The Observer
The business section carries vacancies for sales executives, lawyers, accountants and other professionals; this section also includes editorials related to work and regular special features aimed at particular segments of the labour market.

The Sunday Telegraph
The *Sunday Telegraph* includes a repeat in the City and

Business section of the previous Thursday's 'Telegraph Appointments' supplement.

The Sunday Times
The Sunday Times includes an 18-page broadsheet supplement of professional and executive vacancies and is regarded as the leading source of senior management positions in the £50,000 plus salary bracket. This supplement also includes editorial and job-related issues.

Scottish newspapers
The following list gives an idea of the newspapers available in Scotland, but is not exhaustive. See also the section on Edinburgh on page 114.

Daily Record
Published in Glasgow from Monday to Saturday mornings and sold throughout Scotland, the *Daily Record* advertises all kinds of jobs. The largest situations vacant sections appear on Mondays and Wednesdays.

Sunday Mail
Also published by the *Daily Record*, this paper advertises a variety of jobs each week.

Herald
Published in Glasgow every weekday morning, this national paper has job sections on Tuesdays and Fridays.

Evening Times
This is the *Herald*'s sister paper. It is read mainly in Glasgow and the Strathclyde region and advertises jobs on Mondays, Wednesdays and Fridays.

Sunday Post
Available throughout Scotland and some of northern England, the *Sunday Post* is published in Dundee and carries a range of job advertisements each week.

Aberdeen Press and Journal
This paper is available in the north of Scotland, from Montrose in the south up to Orkney and Shetland in the north, and also in the Western Isles. Its recruitment section is published on Mondays, Wednesdays and Fridays, concentrating on public sector appointments on Wednesdays and on jobs in the oil and gas industries on Fridays.

Dumfries and Galloway Standard
All types of job are advertised on Wednesdays and Fridays. The paper covers the whole of the Dumfries and Galloway region.

Highland News
This is a weekly paper that advertises situations vacant in the Highlands.

Free newspapers in Scotland
Here are just a few of the free Scottish papers to give an idea of what is available.

The Glaswegian
Distributed free of charge to over 200,000 households between Wednesday and Friday each week, this paper includes a wide range of job advertisements.

Aberdeen Herald and Post
This is a weekly free paper which carries advertisements for jobs in the Greater Aberdeen area.

Lanarkshire People
Covering the Motherwell and Hamilton areas, the *Lanarkshire People* has a situations vacant column every week.

Local paid press
The local paid press is an obvious and important source of local vacancies and also often carries details of jobs in other parts of the UK and overseas, particularly those requiring skills associated with local people.

The government-funded survey of employee engagements undertaken in 1992 and described in the introduction to this section showed that nine per cent of jobs at associate professional (technician) level and above were obtained in this way, along with 19 per cent of all other jobs including 23 per cent of part-time and 15 per cent of full-time vacancies.

Local free newspapers

Free newspapers play a much less significant role in recruitment advertising and, according to the 1992 survey mentioned above, only 1.5 per cent of jobs were obtained in this way. They can, however, be a useful source of information for local business news and if, for instance, you are starting up an interesting business, you might be able to get some editorial coverage (and, thereby, free publicity for your service or product). Write yourself a press release and send it to the editor. Send a copy to the paid press too although the free papers seem to be somewhat more hungry for copy.

Finding out about jobs in other areas

Local newspapers are also useful if you want to move to a particular area. If you are not sure which newspapers cover your chosen area(s) you can get this information from either the *Benn's* or *BRAD* directories; these are readily available in most reference libraries. You can then contact the newspaper company to find out which, if any, are the main days for job advertisements (this often tends to be on Thursday evenings) and what arrangements you can make to have copies of the papers mailed to you.

I have chosen four cities in different parts of the UK to illustrate local and regional paid and free newspapers.

Bristol
Paid newspapers

The *Western Daily Press* is published by Bristol United Press Ltd (Tel: 0117-929 7297) and is the regional daily morning newspaper that covers Bristol and Avon, Dorset, Gloucester, Gwent, Hereford, North Devon, Somerset, Wiltshire and Worcester. It accepts a full range of vacancies every day of the week but Thursday is the big day for job advertisements.

The *Bristol Evening Post* is the sister paper to the *Western Daily Press* and covers Bristol and Avon. Job advertisements of all kinds appear throughout the week but mainly on Thursday. Vacancies in the health service tend to appear on Wednesday.

Free newspapers

The local free weekly newspapers are:

- *The Bristol Observer* (Tel: 0117-926 0080)
- *The Bristol Journal* (Tel: 0117-923 1153).

Cambridge
Paid newspapers

The *Cambridge Evening News* is the main source of job advertisements and is published from Monday to Friday by Cambridge Newspapers Ltd (Tel: 01223 358877). It carries job vacancies every day in both the noon and evening editions and includes a special jobs feature on Wednesdays with around 300 advertised vacancies. These include a range of both white and blue collar occupations, including professional and managerial appointments. The paper also carries job-related editorials and a list of the local employment bureaux and recruitment agencies showing their job ranges.

Free newspapers

The *Cambridge Weekly News* is also published by Cambridge Newspapers Ltd on Wednesdays. This is distributed free of charge to local householders and carries about four pages of job vacancies, mainly in catering, industrial, sales and office work.

The *Cambridgeshire Town Crier* is published on Wednesdays. It covers and is distributed to an area of around five miles radius from the centre of Cambridge. It features a general range of local vacancies each week.

Edinburgh
Paid newspapers
If you wanted to move to Edinburgh there are three paid newspapers you could use. These are all produced by Scotsman Publications (Tel: 0131-556 9111).

The *Evening News* is published from Monday to Saturday and carries job vacancies in the Edinburgh and Lothian region, including some professional but mainly office and sales appointments.

The Scotsman is published on weekday mornings and carries a recruitment supplement on Fridays, along with job advertisements in the main body of the paper. These vacancies cover the whole of Scotland but a large proportion are based in Edinburgh. Accountancy, health and welfare, hotel and catering, office work, computing, marketing, sales and media and other professional appointments are included.

Scotland on Sunday also covers the whole of the country and includes the 'Business Week' supplement with news, investigations and analysis of business affairs in Scotland as well as the rest of the UK and abroad. It carries a wide range of professional and other appointments similar to those in *The Scotsman*.

Free newspapers
There are also a number of free weekly newspapers that you might try:

- *North Edinburgh News* (Tel: 0131-332 1236)
- *Tolcross Times* (Tel: 0131-228 3768)

▶ *Western Hailes Sentinel* (Tel: 0131-442 4588)
▶ *Edinburgh Herald and Post* (Tel: 0131-228 5042).

Manchester
Paid newspapers

The *Manchester Evening News* is published by the company of that name (Tel: 0161-832 9191) and carries all types of jobs every day from Monday to Saturday. However, the main nights for job advertisements are as follows:

Tuesday: management, professional, executive, secretarial and clerical.

Wednesday: building and engineering jobs at all levels.

Thursday: sales and marketing and miscellaneous.

Free newspapers

These include *Metro News* which is the sister paper to the *Manchester Evening News* (Tel: 0161-832 9191). Job advertisements are often sold as a package to appear in both newspapers. However, by no means all the advertisements that appear in the *Evening News* are covered in *Metro News*.

The Advertiser is another free weekly newspaper in the Manchester area (Tel: 0161-832 7200).

How to find jobs in your region

Many local newspaper publishers now produce weekly publications – in newspaper format – dedicated to job vacancies in a particular conurbation or region. In addition, there are some which feature several thousand national vacancies, across a wide range of occupations and levels. These include the *Job Hunters Guide*, which is published weekly by EMAP Newspapers Ltd and costs £1, and *Jobsearch*, which is also published weekly by Trinity Newspapers Southern Limited, and costs 95p. Both of these publications present the advertisements in regional order and, in the case of *Jobsearch*, alphabetically by occupation. *Job Hunters Guide* also includes informative features relating to employment issues.

Trade, professional and other periodicals

These publications can be important sources of job vacancies. The government-funded survey in 1992 of over 22,000 appointments showed that about 30 per cent of the following types of vacancy were filled through advertisements in trade and other specialist publications:

- professional occupations
- professional associate/technical occupations
- management/administrative occupations.

The overall market share, covering all types of vacancy, was 11 per cent and was particularly high in the public sector in London and the south-east. On the other hand, only one per cent of manual jobs was filled in this way.

Where to find these journals

About 200 of the publications most heavily involved in job advertising are listed in the quick reference guide under the relevant job titles. The telephone number of the publisher is included in each case as, whilst most of the titles are readily available from newsagents, some are not.

The *BRAD Directory* (British Rates and Data), which is revised monthly, lists over 3,000 such publications. *Benn's Directory* also includes this list. One or both of these directories may be available in your local reference or business library. Whilst neither reference book clarifies the position as regards job advertising, it might be worth investigating the titles most obviously associated with your line of work – particularly if you have free access to these in the library. Alternatively you could ring the publisher direct.

Read between the lines!

It is worth looking at some of these publications in more detail. Whilst in some journals the range of job advertisements is clearly reflected in the titles, for example *Accounting Technician* and *Architects Journal*, in others both the range of occupations and the number of advertisements are much greater than you might suppose. Here are six examples of professional journals whose scope is wider than you might think.

Artists Newsletter

Artists Newsletter is published monthly by Arctic Producers Publishing Company Ltd (Tel: 0191-567 3589) at £1.95. It reflects the reality that long-term jobs related to fine arts tend to be confined to education. Thus the job advertisements are mainly for art teachers, arts administrators, fellowships including teaching responsibilities, art department technicians, clerical support staff, museum and art gallery workers. More interestingly, the newsletter highlights an alternative way of working; it includes invitations for artists to tender for specific fixed periods in public art projects. In one edition a local authority was looking for an artist to make and install wall designs, another for someone to work on the design team of a new hospital block and another to work with the borough architect on the design of a new school and associated landscaping.

Caterer and Hotelkeeper

Caterer and Hotelkeeper is published weekly by Reed Business Publishing (Tel: 0181-652 8310) and costs £1.45. It features around 150 vacancies each week. Whilst the majority of these are for people with backgrounds in catering and hotelkeeping management and/or the cooking and serving of food, some would be suitable for people from other industries, including accountants, book-keepers, building services managers and personnel officers.

Vacancies are included for couples to manage jointly various types of catering outlet and opportunities for trainees who have recently completed full-time courses are also featured. Catering businesses are offered for sale, ranging from tea shops for lease at around £30,000 to hotels for sale at £1,000,000 or more.

The Grocer

The Grocer is published weekly by William Reed Publishing Ltd (Tel: 01293 613156) and costs 40p. Each edition carries around 40 A4 pages of job advertisements including senior appointments in the £50,000 plus salary range. This magazine is also much used by recruitment consultants to publicise their clients' vacancies.

As you would expect, a large proportion of the jobs are connected with food retailing and include vacancies for graduate trainees, account managers, area sales executives, buyers, merchandising development executives, product managers, regional account executives, sales and marketing directors, representatives and trainees, retail and shopping centre managers and territory managers.

The Grocer also has an established reputation in other industries and covers advertisements in the categories shown above over a wide range of products as diverse as art tiles, broadcasting equipment, business gifts, cables, clinical waste, coach operating services, electronics, flags and banners, office interiors, pharmaceuticals, rubber mouldings and weigh, wrap and labelling equipment.

The Health Service Journal

The Health Service Journal is published weekly by Macmillan Magazines Ltd (Tel: 0171-836 6633) and costs £1.50. Each edition includes about 20 A4 pages of job advertisements preceded, usefully, by an alphabetical index of the job titles covered. It deals with management/administrative professional advisory jobs in the health service rather than those involving direct patient care. Whilst in many cases a nursing or medical background is a prerequisite for these jobs, others would be suitable for people who have gained relevant experience elsewhere in either the public or private sectors. Jobs in the latter category include accountants and accountancy technicians, building managers, building surveyors, buyers, catering managers, computer experts, engineering officers, energy managers, estate managers, IT project managers, librarians and personnel and human resources managers.

Nature
Nature is published weekly by Macmillan Magazines Ltd (Tel: 0171-872 0104) at £4.50 and is regarded by many as the world's foremost scientific journal. Each week it carries about 150 opportunities throughout the world across the full spectrum of scientific disciplines, including jobs in industry and academia.

The Stage
The Stage is another interesting example. It is published weekly by The Stage Newspaper Limited (Tel: 0171-403 1818) and costs 60p. As well as the sort of vacancies you would expect – from actors to acrobats, dancers to drummers – it advertises jobs that performers can do during periods of 'resting'. These jobs might be of interest to you too if you are looking for temporary work – you don't need an Equity card! Some reflect the skills normally associated with performing including sales/demonstrating, fund-raising, life modelling; others – such as sandwich-making and courier/delivery work – do not.

Executive Post
Of course, the content of many publications is clearly signalled by their titles. *Executive Post*, which is published monthly, advertises professional, executive and managerial posts and franchising opportunities and includes a wide range of features on related issues. It is available by subscription from:

Executive Post
631 Chesterfield Road
Sheffield
South Yorkshire S8 0RX
Tel: 0114-255 5040
Fax: 0114-250 7135

Source of speculative submissions

These publications can be a valuable source of information about what is happening in your industry and can guide you towards speculative approaches. Remember that 13 per cent of all vacancies in the categories mentioned above, and 18 per cent of other types of job, are filled in this way.

BBC television and radio

The BBC Education Directorate produces a wide range of programmes for radio and television related to jobs, careers, education, training and enterprise. At the time of writing these include the following:

Job Bank: a BBC2 series providing information for college leavers and showing young people at work in a variety of jobs.

Business Matters: a BBC2 feature looking at how to keep up with the rapid changes that are taking place in the business world.

The Business: a series of documentaries on BBC2 that examines the organisations, strategies and experiences of a range of businesses in this country and abroad.

Second Chances: a one-week campaign on BBC1 to encourage and give direction to adults to return to learning. Concentrated over one week each year, it forms part of a major initiative for adult learners also involving ITV, Channel 4 and the cable TV companies.

Many other relevant issues are covered in these and other broadcast programmes and in the written and audio-visual materials that are produced and sold by the BBC (including programmes about working abroad, which are described in chapter 8). Full details of all these services are contained in a free booklet called *On Course* which is published four times a year. Your name can be added to the mailing list by writing to:

Subscriptions
On Course
Room G420
BBC White City
London W12 7TS
Tel: 0181-746 1111

Independent television

The Jobfinder service

The independent television companies work with the Employment Service to provide the Jobfinder service. This includes the transmission of regional and European vacancies which have been notified to the Jobcentres – plus other work-related information. These programmes are usually transmitted in the early morning but you can, of course, record them. The times will be shown in your newspaper or TV listings magazine.

Although Jobfinder's prime objective is to serve the needs of unemployed people, it has a wider remit which is stated to be to enable the adult population as a whole to maximise its contribution to the regional economy.

To take one independent company as an example, Central Television, which serves over nine million people, transmits computer pages with details of 30–50 regional and European vacancies each weekday morning – along with a further 10–20 pages of more general employment-related advice and information.

In addition, there is a daily studio-based features section which contains interviews and material shot on location. At least seven different initiatives and organisations are featured each weekday including training schemes, education courses, enterprise initiatives, advice about job-hunting techniques, related publications and recruitment drives – virtually anything that is of interest if you are looking for work or making career choices.

The Jobfinder team also regularly produces booklets and factsheets on employment and enterprise issues, recruitment drives, events, open days and training courses. These can be obtained from:

Support Services
Jobfinder
Central Television
Broad Street
Birmingham B1 2JP
Tel: 0121-634 4265/4630/4586
Fax: 0121-634 4961

If you live in Central's area they would also like to hear from you if you have been involved in a successful enterprise venture. This could, incidentally, provide you with excellent free publicity for your products or service.

Teletext
Information on job vacancies is broadcast through the ITV/Channel 4 Teletext service. Details of vacancies being handled by some private employment agencies, including jobs in computing, begin at page 640. Page 649 repeats details of the Jobcentre vacancies featured in the Jobfinder service on ITV. Advice about benefits, careers and other job-related topics begins on page 650.

Information for speculative submissions
News programmes – both national and regional – along with other current affairs broadcasts, for example *The Money Programme*, can provide you with excellent information about what is happening in the business world – and therefore indicate where you might target your speculative job applications.

8 Vacancies Abroad

The purpose of this chapter

This chapter is intended to get you thinking about whether working abroad would be a viable proposition for you. It presents some of the pros and cons, describes some of the opportunities and points you towards other sources of information to enable you to build up a complete picture of what it is like to live and work overseas.

Why work abroad?

There is something eternally appealing about living abroad. For many people this is an end in itself and, within reason, they don't really mind how they earn their living once they get there. So if you're young – or even if you're mature – and fancy-free you could follow their example and just go. Perhaps, however, you should finish reading this chapter first!

For other people, working abroad has been the means to an end – to make more money than they could in the UK. This has been a particular attraction of working in the Middle East. However, these appointments are not likely to be as plentiful in future.

If you have career and/or family commitments there are a lot of things you need to consider.

The implications of working abroad

There are a number of questions you need to ask yourself:

▶ Where would I be prepared to work and for how long?
▶ What sort of work could I do abroad?
▶ Could I follow my normal occupation?

- What could I expect to earn and what would this mean in real terms?
- What would the cost of living be?
- What taxes would I have to pay?
- What would I be giving up in work terms by going abroad such as career prospects, security and pension rights?
- How easy would it be to re-establish myself in work if and when I decided to return to the UK?
- How would my partner, family and others be affected? Could I and should I take my family with me?
- What are the living conditions like? Are these likely to be acceptable to me and my family?
- What would be the implications of leaving my partner and/or family in the UK?
- What educational provision would be available?
- What are the job prospects for my spouse or any other people who may accompany me?
- What are the potential hazards (climate, political, military) and health implications?
- What health facilities are available and at what cost?

Get a contract

If you are offered a job you need to be sure exactly what the employer will provide in terms of the duration of the contract, salary package, fares, health insurance, superannuation, accommodation, help with your family's education and any other allowances. In other words, you want an intelligible written contract that you should discuss with your legal adviser.

Answering these questions

The rest of this chapter attempts to help you to answer these questions, mainly by pointing you in the direction of the other relevant sources of information. But first, it might set things in context to provide some figures.

Some facts and figures

There are apparently about three million British expatriates; in 1992, 216,000 people left Great Britain. Of these, 57,000 went to countries of the European Union, 73,000 to the Commonwealth and the remainder to other countries. However, only about a quarter – 54,000 in 1992 – took up specific job appointments. The rest were made up of the workers' families, people retiring overseas and so on.

A declining market?

At the time of writing it appears that, in general, there are not as many job opportunities as there used to be (and that also applies to the EC in spite of easier entry conditions). Because of the employment situation in their own countries more people are chasing the jobs available and employers don't therefore need to offer such generous packages. At one time qualified engineers and other highly trained professionals in short supply could expect flights and accommodation to be provided for their families, along with school fees, medical care and a range of other perks. Now, except in the case of senior appointments, single status contracts are more usual.

In addition, there have been well-publicised instances of Britons being duped by bogus employment agencies. In one instance, agencies were charging fees to put building craftsmen in touch with jobs in the Gulf – vacancies that in reality would be filled by the much cheaper labour available from the Indian subcontinent. This has led to newspapers being cautious about dealing with jobs abroad and they now all claim to vet prospective employers thoroughly before accepting their advertisements.

There have been other instances where British workers

have been encouraged to go abroad only to find that their skill levels were not accepted in the other country. You can now get advice about craft skill equivalents from the Department of Employment and from the DTI in relation to professional qualifications.

Still a demand for the right skills

Nevertheless, over the world as a whole, the less technically advanced nations will inevitably want to draw on the skills of those that have progressed further in this respect. Provided we are not priced out of the market, there will continue to be opportunities for Britons with the right qualifications to find work abroad. You will know how well advanced you are in your own field and therefore whether you are likely to have something to offer in other countries.

You can, in any case, check whether your skills are in demand by looking at the vacancies that appear in the national press (☞ chapter 7 to see when and where particular types of vacancies are advertised). Your professional or trade journal should also be helpful in this respect (☞ chapter 7). In addition, there are a number of publications specialising in jobs abroad which will also show whether your skills are in demand.

Working in the European Community

Rights and conditions as a UK national

As a UK national you have the right to live and work in another member state of the European Community without a work permit, i.e. in Belgium, Denmark, France, Greece, Germany, Italy, Luxembourg, the Netherlands, the Republic of Ireland, Spain and Portugal. You may, however, need other documentation and will have to check with the embassy concerned. You will have the same rights as nationals of that country with regard to pay, working conditions, access to housing, vocational training, social security and trade union membership. Your family is entitled to join you and enjoy similar rights.

Learn the language

Things can, however, be very difficult if you don't speak the language. Even in the Netherlands, where you expect almost everyone to speak English, you may still be faced with completing tax returns in Dutch!

There are many courses available in foreign language training and your first port of call might be your local library to find out what the local FE colleges provide. The BBC also broadcasts programmes and produces a series of audio-visual packages. Details can be obtained from the address given below under the section Help from the BBC. (☛ chapter 7 to find out about relevant broadcasts on TV and radio.)

If you are in a hurry, a much more costly option would be to undertake an intensive course with a specialist language school. These are widely advertised in the general and trade press. You should obtain their brochures and compare what each has to offer.

Help from the Employment Department

The public employment services of the 12 member states of the European Community are, by EC regulation, committed to work together to enable job-seekers within the Community to have freedom of movement when looking for work.

In Britain this responsibility is given to the Overseas Placing Unit of the Employment Department. You can contact the Unit through your local Jobcentre. Staff there will undertake a search for you of the overseas vacancies (in the EC and elsewhere) held on their national vacancy data system (known as NATVACS). They will also be able to give you further information about the overseas vacancies – again, in the EC and elsewhere – that are advertised on page 649 of Channel 4's Teletext service (☛ chapter 7 for more information about this service). You will need to give them the reference number displayed on the particular vacancy. In both cases they will tell you how to apply for these vacancies, which is usually by completing their form ES 13.

The Overseas Placing Unit has also produced a series of 12 booklets. One is about working abroad in general, each of the others is about working in a particular EC member state. You can obtain copies of these from your local Jobcentre.

Information about specific trades and professions

In addition, the Unit holds information on seeking work overseas in specific trades and professions. This can be obtained by writing direct to the Unit giving details of the type of work you are looking for and the countries where you want to work. The address of the Overseas Placing Unit is:

Employment Service
Overseas Placing Unit
Steel City House
c/o Rockingham House
123 West Street
Sheffield
South Yorkshire S1 4ER

Comparability between British and overseas qualifications

The Employment Department produces information sheets to help you compare qualifications for skilled craft workers in a range of industries, including hotel and catering, construction and agriculture. For further details contact:

The Comparability Co-ordinator
Employment Department
Qualifications and Standards Branch
Moorfoot
Sheffield
South Yorkshire S1 4PQ
Tel: 0114-259 4144

The Department of Trade and Industry (DTI) provides information on the comparability of professional qualifications abroad. You need to ask for their booklet *Europe Open for Professionals*.

The DTI can also provide you with a European Community Certificate of Experience if you have gained the necessary experience in your particular area of work. You have to pay a fee for this. For information in either case, contact:

Department of Trade and Industry
Ashdown House
123 Victoria Street
London SW1E 6RB
Tel: 0171-215 5000

Employment agencies and recruitment consultants

A list of agencies dealing with work in the EC and elsewhere can be obtained by writing to:

The Federation of Recruitment and Employment
  Services Ltd
36–38 Mortimer Street
London W1N 7RB

Information about executive recruiting agencies in over 65 countries can be found in *Executive Grapevine Volume 2: The International Directory of Recruitment Consultants*. This includes industry and functional specialisations, remuneration levels, methodology of assignments, fees and guarantees and features the major search networks.

This volume may be available in your local library or, failing that, more information can be obtained from the publishers:

Executive Grapevine International Limited
4 Theobald Court
Theobald Street
Borehamwood
Hertfordshire WD6 4RN
Tel: 0181-953 9939
Fax: 0181-953 9808

☛ the section on private recruitment and employment agencies in chapter 6.

Information about working for the European Commission itself can be obtained by writing to:

Recruitment, Appointments and Promotion Division
DG1X
Commission of European Communities
22 rue de la Roi
B-1049 Brussels
Belgium

Specific job opportunities

As discussed above, details of specific vacancies can be found in the press and other media. It is clearly not possible to provide detailed information here about what jobs are likely to be available. Nor is it desirable, for, at the time of writing, there is considerable uncertainty as to what point individual countries have reached on the recession cycle. The job situation could change quickly and significantly. It may, however, be appropriate to quote one particular example here.

Teaching English as a foreign language

If you feel that you can put yourself across to people in an effective and interesting way, have a sound grasp of the way the English language works and want to see the world, you may want to consider teaching English as a foreign language. As well as an existing high demand for this skill in Europe, it is estimated that Eastern Europe and the new Russian republics will require 100,000 native English speakers to teach the language over the next five years. It is a job which you can do freelance or with an organisation like the British Council (address below). You can work with groups or individuals and normally have control over how long you want to do the job and the hours you want to work. This job could take you all over the non-English-speaking world or allow you to settle in one spot – provided there were enough potential students around. (There are also opportunities to teach English to overseas students in private language schools in this country.)

Details of specific vacancies are advertised in the specialist overseas job journals described below. Information about job opportunities and details of courses in teaching English as a foreign language can be obtained by writing to:

The British Council
English Language Information Section
4th Floor
Medlo Street
Manchester M15 4AA

For details of the syllabus of the RSA Certificate in Teaching English as a Foreign Language and a list of training centres, contact:

TEFL Unit
University of Cambridge Local Examinations
Syndicate Buildings (UCLES)
1 Hills Road
Cambridge CB1 2EU
Tel: 01223 61111

Seasonal and casual work abroad

There are a number of books about working abroad on a casual or seasonal basis that should be readily available in bookshops and/or libraries. Some long-established titles include *Working Holidays*, *Summer Jobs Abroad* and *Work Your Way Around the World*.

Other sources of information about jobs abroad

Specialist periodicals
Overseas Jobs Express: published fortnightly and distributed by paid subscription, carries job vacancies and editorial on international employment and related issues; immigration, travel, finance, health, leisure, international lifestyle. It also markets a wide range of publications about all aspects of working abroad, including specific countries. For further details, contact:

Overseas Jobs Express
Premier House
Shoreham Airport
Sussex BN1 5FF
Tel: 01273 440220
Fax: 01273 440229

Jobs in Europe and Jobs International: a monthly magazine, available on subscription, features articles related to working abroad, jobs and employment bureaux specialising in overseas vacancies. It markets a wide range of related publications and runs an advice line called EURO BURO. You can obtain further information from:

Jobs in Europe and Jobs International
52 Queens Gardens
London W2 3AA
Tel: 0171-724 5346

Overseas vacancies advertised in national newspapers
The European: published every Thursday in Britain, includes an Executive Search category which carries senior executive vacancies and educational advertising related to the EC. It also includes features on work and education, including graduate opportunities in the EC.

The Guardian: carries an international appointments feature, on Tuesdays, which includes positions abroad in both UK and international companies. It also carries recruitment advertising from the French recruitment publication *Carrières et Emplois*, and the leading Danish newspaper, *Politiken*.

Help from the BBC

The BBC broadcasts a number of relevant programmes on both radio and television which at the time of writing includes language teaching on Radio 3 and a BBC2 series about how businesses operate in some other EC countries called *Italy means Business* and *Germany means Business*. Further details of these and other programmes and related audio-visual packages are contained in the BBC's *On Course* booklet; you can get the latest edition and be added to the mailing list by writing to:

On Course
Room G420
BBC White City
London W12 7TS
Tel: 0181-746 1111

Reading list

There is a wide range of titles which you will probably want to research in your library or bookshop. These include:

A Year Off... A Year On?, Suzanne Straw, Hobsons Publishing PLC
For anyone planning a constructive break, either between stages of education or between jobs. It contains all the

essential application details and is divided into sections on Great Britain, abroad and developing countries.

Directory of Jobs and Careers Abroad, Alex Lipinski, Vacation Work
Covers a broad spectrum of work abroad, from two-week work camps in Europe to two-year contracts in the Middle East to permanent emigration to New Zealand.

Nexus Expatriate Magazine, a monthly magazine available on enrolment to the Expat Network, covering all aspects of working abroad and including several hundred job adverts, concentrating on the Middle East.

Expat Network
Carolyn House
5th Floor
Dingwell Road
Croydon
Surrey CR0 4NZ
Tel: 0181-760 5100

Working Abroad, Godfrey Golzen and Margaret Stewart, Kogan Page Ltd
A general guide to moving, living and working abroad covering some 40 countries, including Europe, Africa, the Middle East, the Americas, Asia and Australia.

Working Abroad: Personal money management for the UK expatriate, Peter Gartland, FT Business Information Ltd
This publication deals with UK tax liability, investments, insurance, pension schemes, letting your property in the UK and educating your children abroad.

9 Graduate Vacancies

The purpose of this chapter

This chapter is intended to help you as a student or someone who has graduated fairly recently to:

▶ identify the trends in graduate recruitment
▶ locate the sources of relevant vacancies
▶ consider what you can do to make yourself more appealing to potential employers
▶ broaden your vision of the opportunities that are available to you to establish a foothold in the job market.

The other parts of this handbook apply equally to graduates as to other adults and may, indeed, be more relevant if you graduated some time ago.

Graduate unemployment

At the peak of the recent recession, in 1992, 12 per cent of that year's graduates were still unemployed six months after completing their degree courses. In 1993 that figure fell to eight per cent although this was in large part due to students adjusting to the economic situation. For example, many of them stayed on at university in order to increase their appeal to employers by gaining knowledge in one particular vocational area. Only about one in three of the graduating population found jobs quickly.

Future job prospects for graduates

It is important to note, however, that throughout the recent recession, unemployment amongst graduates as a whole remained significantly lower than for the rest of the population. And that trend is likely to increase in future years as jobs become more complex and highly skilled.

Also, after previous recessions, newly qualified graduates have fared better than other candidates in the labour market. In fact, various studies concluded that, in 1994, employers would increase their recruitment of graduates by between seven and 16 per cent on the previous year. It was predicted that this would be followed by a further substantial increase in 1995.

Nevertheless, it is important to remember that there will also be more graduates chasing these jobs. It is equally important not to think your degree was a waste of time from a career point of view. Whatever difficulties you are likely to experience in finding satisfying work the opportunities are, in future, likely to be far more limited for your contemporaries who have not undertaken higher education.

Where do graduates go to work and what do they do?

People graduating in 1993 went into the following types of organisation:

- 19.8% commerce
- 19.1% local government and the National Health Service
- 9.0% industry (excluding engineering)
- 7.9% engineering industry
- 6.7% education
- 6.5% accountancy
- 5.8% banking and insurance
- 4.8% Civil Service and armed forces
- 4.7% public utilities
- 3.8% building and civil engineering
- 12.3% others.

Graduates were employed to do the following types of job:

- 21.0% medical/personnel/security

- 13.5% science and engineering
- 12.6% finance
- 10.8% administration and operational management
- 8.6% buying, selling, marketing
- 7.2% computing and management services
- 4.6% environment, building, surveying
- 4.0% creative, entertainment
- 3.9% teaching, lecturing
- 2.1% library, information work
- 11.7% other.

What major graduate employers offer

Commerce
A fifth of all new graduates now start their career in commerce. This covers a broad range of services including retailing, employment agencies, advertising, software houses and consultants, publishers, exhibition organisers and market researchers – in fact any organisation which provides services, rather than manufactures goods, on a commercial basis. They offer a range of jobs from program designers to commissioning editors, account executives to marketing managers.

Health service and local government
Health and local government are the other main recruiters of graduates. As well as those involved directly in patient care – nurses, doctors, dentists, occupational therapists and others – the National Health Service has many jobs in laboratories and administration. Local authorities offer jobs in accountancy, architecture, legal work, arts administration, museums, social work, librarianship, town planning and many others. An increasing number of services are being contracted out from local authorities to commercial firms and consultants. So, if you join, you've got to be prepared for a rapidly changing scene.

Central government

Central government is changing rapidly too. The Civil Service has been drastically pruned during recent years and the cuts are still going on. Departments are being broken down into the Whitehall policy sections and agencies which put agreed plans into action. There are over 200 recruiting sections within the Civil Service – the full list, including addresses, is available from your university careers service. Most graduates begin as executive officers and around 150 each year become administrative trainees to be groomed for the top jobs. An increasing number join the lowest grades of either administrative officer or administrative assistant. In the past some people have risen from these to senior ranks but it remains to be seen whether this will happen in future.

The Civil Service also offers many specialist jobs such as statisticians, lawyers, economists, information officers, architects and accountants.

Despite cuts, opportunities still arise in defence, some with the armed forces and others in government laboratories. Police forces throughout the country have for a long time extensively recruited graduates. Fire and rescue and ambulance services are also increasingly entering the market.

The many quangos (quasi-autonomous non-governmental organisations) are also an important source of jobs. They include organisations such as the National Audit Office, the Health and Audit Commission and the Health and Safety Executive.

Engineering

Engineers were once in great demand but have suffered through the reduction in defence-related jobs. Telecommunications and information technology have come through the recession and opportunities in these disciplines are growing again. Competition in areas such as telephone services, cable television, gas supply, television programme production and the multimedia aspects of computing should create more opportunities.

Jobs abroad

Only about four per cent of people who graduated in 1993 went abroad to work or study. Teaching English as a foreign language (TEFL) is a popular choice amongst those who wish to spend just a short time abroad.

☛ chapter 8 for information about working abroad, including TEFL.

Self-employment

Normally people are advised to get experience and training with an employer before setting up on their own. However, in some instances, for example, if you want to make your living in the creative arts, self-employment may be your main or only outlet.

☛ chapter 5 for information about setting up in business.

How to find out about potential employers

Your university careers service

If you are a recent graduate your first port of call is likely to be your university careers service. They will have an extensive range of information about jobs and training. You can normally make an appointment to see one of the advisers or just drop into the careers library.

If you have moved away from your university town there are reciprocal arrangements to enable you to get advice from your nearest university careers service.

The milkround

Employer participation in the 'milkround' is falling rapidly. A survey of 81 university careers offices showed that for every 100 employer bookings on the milkround in 1990–91, just 38 were made in 1994 at the old universities and 24 at the former polytechnics. This was apparently partly prompted by the lack of student interest. Employers with jobs on offer reported that students were cowed into believing it was impossible to get a job. It's still worth finding out from your careers service which companies will be visiting your university next time round and applying to those that interest you.

Careers fairs

Employers take stands at these events to exhibit the career opportunities they have to offer. It gives you a chance to meet employers' representatives face to face in an informal situation, and you can compare one with another.

There are two kinds of careers fairs: those which concentrate on giving you information about employers and those which are primarily a recruitment exercise. Inevitably both activities occur at all fairs, but the emphasis is slightly different.

A few universities hold specialist fairs which concentrate on specific subjects but most cover the whole range of opportunities in one event. Find out from your careers service what is being planned in your university.

Other ways you can contact potential employers

Many industrial and commercial firms and the Civil Service are decentralising their recruitment drives. Employers are increasingly targeting their recruitment efforts at a few institutions. They are now more likely to seek prospective employees from their local university, than by trawling through the country. Therefore, if you would like to live in a particular area, you will need to apply directly to firms in that area.

☛ chapter 4 for tips on how to find out about and apply directly to firms that you consider may have suitable vacancies.
☛ the Introduction to Part 2 for an overview of the sources of job vacancies.
☛ chapter 10 for an alphabetical quick reference guide to all these sources.

Other sources of graduate vacancies

There is a range of publications which provide information about employers who recruit graduates. These will be available in Universities' Careers Service libraries and include the following items:

GET (Graduate Employment and Training) and GO (Graduate Opportunities): these commercial graduate directories are produced each year in October at the beginning of the recruitment year. As sources of information they are out of date by June, but can be used as a guide to major employers of graduates.

Prospects Directory: the annual graduate directory produced on behalf of the Universities' Careers Services and contains similar information to that in *GET* and *GO*.

Hobsons' Casebooks: these are produced annually by Hobsons Publishing PLC under licence for CRAC (the Careers Research and Advisory Centre). Each publication includes case-studies which give a flavour of life and work in a particular career area along with details of potential employers. The series includes editions on engineering, finance, information technology, law, management, marketing, retailing and sales, racial equality, science and working women.

Prospects Today: a list of immediate vacancies produced by the Central Services Unit (CSU) for Universities' Careers Services and used widely by employers. It can be obtained through your university careers service or direct from:

CSU
Armstrong House
Oxford Road
Manchester M1 7ED
Tel: 0161-236 9816

Prospects for the Finalist: provides details of vacancies which will be available the following summer/autumn. It is produced at intervals by CSU and is available from them direct (see above) or through your university careers service.

Not sure what you want to do?

You should certainly contact your university careers service for guidance. There is reliable research to show that, because of technological advances, people will have to make substantial changes to the direction of their career several times during their working lives. All-age careers guidance will need to become an essential part of that process. Unfortunately, at the present time, vocational guidance is not readily available for most adults in many parts of the country. You are fortunate as a graduate to have the opportunity, so use it if you need it!

Know what you want but can't get it?

If this describes your situation there are a number of tactics you might try.

Be more open-minded
One option is to consider taking a more junior position than you would ideally like when looking for your first job. Get a foothold in the sector of your choice and work hard. In this way you will soon be noticed and better opportunities will come your way. For example, the BBC is renowned for the number of its producers and directors

who began as production assistants, researchers and secretaries! Don't reject jobs which may seem below your capabilities when they may provide opportunities for you to make the first step on your ladder to a successful career.

Broaden your horizons

An alternative is to try for work in a less sought-after sector. Transport, warehousing and distribution are often neglected by graduate job-seekers, but have much to offer. Employment related to leisure, such as cinema management, supervision of sports and fitness centres, bingo halls and betting shops, is increasing. The tourist trade continues to develop and retailing has begun to expand again too.

Postgraduate studies or training

Another possibility is to continue in further education or training that would make you more attractive to a potential employer. Once again, your university careers service should be able to provide you with information and advice.

Other sources of help with jobs

Along with everyone else, graduates are entitled to use Jobcentres to find jobs, together with the other services that they provide to help people to get back into work. In some of the larger conurbations they also run Jobclubs specifically for graduates.

☛ chapter 6 for further details of Jobcentre services.

Getting help from TECs and LECs

Your local Training and Enterprise Council (TEC), in England or Wales, or your Local Enterprise Company (LEC), in Scotland, may have a scheme to help graduates into work. In Bradford and Sheffield, for instance, the TECs and the old universities together run versions of what was once a national programme called Graduate

Gateway. The idea is to give graduates the opportunity to gain practical experience by working for a small company. In return that company gets the benefit of the graduate's expertise. Graduates may also be given a short period of training at a business school prior to joining the firm.

Involvement in this scheme has convinced many small firms of the value of employing graduates where there had previously been only scepticism. For example, a cutlery firm in Sheffield made strenuous efforts to retain the services of a female philosophy graduate whose training in clear thinking proved invaluable and who came their way through this scheme.

☞ the list of the addresses and telephone numbers of TECs and LECs in the annex to chapter 5.

Getting additional information about specific careers

This may be obtained by writing to the relevant professional body in the list set out as an annex to chapter 2.

10 Quick Reference Guide: Job Advertisements in the Press

The purpose of this chapter

This chapter will provide a quick reference to vacancies appearing in the national press – including daily and Sunday newspapers – covering over 300 occupations and more than 200 publications.

The list shows the frequency of publication – unless this is obvious from the title – and, in the case of daily publications, the day(s) of the week when the particular type of vacancy appears. The publishers' telephone numbers are also included, which should be particularly useful for locating the less well-known publications.

Title	Frequency	Telephone
ACCOUNT DIRECTORS		
Campaign	weekly	0171-413 5479
Marketing	weekly	0171-413 4337
ACCOUNT EXECUTIVES		
Campaign	weekly	0171-413 5479
The Grocer	weekly	01293 613400
Marketing	weekly	0171-413 4337
PR Week	weekly	0171-413 4543
ACCOUNT MANAGERS		
Campaign	weekly	0171-413 5479
Daily Express	Thursday	0171-928 8000
The Grocer	weekly	01293 613400
Marketing	weekly	0171-413 4337
Printing World	weekly	01732 364422
PR Week	weekly	0171-413 4543
Sunday Times		0171-782 7000
Times	Thursday	0171-782 7000

Title	Frequency	Telephone
ACCOUNTANTS		
Accountancy	monthly	0171-833 3291
Accountancy Age	weekly	0171-637 4242
Caterer and Hotelkeeper	weekly	0181-652 8380
Certified Accountant	monthly	00 353 21 313855
Daily Telegraph	Thursday	0171-538 5000
Economist	monthly	0171-830 7000
Financial Times	Thursday	0171-873 3000
Guardian	Tues & Sat	0171-278 2332
Health Service Journal	weekly	0171-836 6633
Independent	Tues & Thurs	0171-253 1222
Independent on Sunday		0171-251-1251
Jobsearch	weekly	01753 532041
Local Government Chronicle	weekly	0171-837 1212
Management Accounting	monthly	0171-637 2311
Public Finance	weekly	0171-895 8823
Sunday Telegraph		0171-538 5000
Sunday Times		0171-782 7000
Times Higher Education Supplement	weekly	0171-782 3000
ACCOUNTING TECHNICIANS		
Accounting Technician	monthly	0181-624 8244
Daily Telegraph	Thursday	0171-538 5000
Health Service Journal	weekly	0171-240 1101
Jobsearch	weekly	01753 532041
Local Government Chronicle	Thursday	0171-837 1212
ACTORS		
Stage	weekly	0171-403 1818
ACTUARIES		
Money Management	monthly	0171-405 6969
Observer	Sunday	0171-278 2332
Times	Monday	0171-782 7000

Title	Frequency	Telephone
ACUPUNCTURISTS		
Journal of Alternative and Complementary Medicine	monthly	01932 874333
ADVERTISING		
Guardian	Monday	0171-278 2332
Independent on Sunday		0171-251 1251
AEROBICS AND FITNESS INSTRUCTORS		
Health and Fitness	monthly	0171-388 3171
Leisure Opportunities	weekly	01462 431385
AERONAUTICAL ENGINEERING TECHNICIANS		
Daily Telegraph	Tues & Thurs	0171-538 5000
Engineering News	monthly	
Flight International	Wednesday	0181-652 3500
AEROSPACE ENGINEERS		
Flight International	weekly	0181-652 3500
Sunday Telegraph		0171-538 5000
AGRICULTURAL SCIENTISTS		
Farmers Weekly	weekly	0181-652 4030
Times Higher Education Supplement	weekly	0171-782 3232
AGRONOMISTS		
Farmers Weekly	weekly	0181-652 4030
New Scientist	weekly	0171-261 7309
ANTHROPOLOGISTS		
Times Higher Education Supplement	weekly	0171-782 3232
ARBORICULTURE		
Opportunities	weekly	0181-667 6000

Title	Frequency	Telephone

ARCHAEOLOGISTS
Guardian	Friday	0171-278 2332
Museums Journal and Recruitment Supplement	monthly	0171-333 1731
Planning	weekly	01452 417553

ARCHITECTS
Architects Journal	weekly	0171-837 1212
Building Design	weekly	0181-855 7777
Guardian	Tuesday	0171-278 2332
Independent	Wednesday	0171-253 1222
Jobsearch	fortnightly	01753 532041
Planning	weekly	01452 417553
RIBA Journal	monthly	0171-537 2222
Sunday Telegraph	weekly	0171-538 5000
Times	Thursday	0171-782 7000
Times Higher Education Supplement	weekly	0171-782 3000

ARCHITECTURAL TECHNICIANS
Building Design	weekly	0181-855 7777

ART AND DESIGN TEACHERS: SECONDARY
Times Educational Supplement	weekly	0171-782 3232

ART AND DESIGN TEACHERS: UNIVERSITY AND FURTHER EDUCATION
Artists Newsletter	weekly	0191-567 3589
Guardian	Tuesday	0171-278 2332
Times Educational Supplement	weekly	0171-782 3232
Times Higher Education Supplement	weekly	0171-782 3000

ART DIRECTORS
Campaign	weekly	0171-413 5479
Marketing	weekly	0171-413 4337

Title	Frequency	Telephone
ART TECHNICIANS		
Artists Newsletter	weekly	0191-567 3589
ARTISTS		
Artists Newsletter	weekly	0191-567 3589
Arts Management Weekly		0171-333 1733
Guardian	Monday	0171-278 2332
ARTWORKERS		
Campaign	weekly	0171-413 5479
Marketing	weekly	0171-413 4337
ARTS ADMINISTRATORS		
Artists Newsletter	monthly	0191-567 3589
Arts Management Weekly		0171-333 2332
Classical Music	fortnightly	0171-333 1742
Guardian	Mon & Sat	0171-278 2332
Stage	weekly	0171-403 1818
Times	Tuesday	0171-782 7000
AU PAIRS		
The Lady	weekly	0171-379 4717
AUDIO-VISUAL ENGINEERS		
Audio Visual	monthly	0181-688 7788
AUTOMOBILE ENGINEERS		
Engineer	weekly	0181-855 7777
Sunday Telegraph		0171-538 5000
BANK MANAGERS		
Guardian	Saturday	0171-278 2332
Independent on Sunday		0171-251 1251
BAR STAFF		
Caterer and Hotelkeeper	weekly	0181-652 8380

BARRISTERS see LAWYERS

BEAUTICIANS see also MAKE-UP ARTISTS, THEATRICAL

Time Out	weekly	0171-813 6004

Title	Frequency	Telephone
BEAUTY THERAPISTS		
Times Educational Supplement	weekly	0171-782 3232
BENEFITS OFFICERS (social welfare and housing)		
Opportunities	weekly	0181-667 6000
BIOCHEMISTS		
Daily Telegraph	Thursday	0171-538 5000
Nature	weekly	0171-836 6633
BIOLOGISTS		
Daily Telegraph	Mon & Thurs	0171-538 5000
Guardian	Tuesday	0171-278 2332
Nature	weekly	0171-836 6633
New Scientist	weekly	0171-261 7309
Sunday Times		0171-782 7000
Times	Thursday	0171-782 7000
Times Educational Supplement	weekly	0171-782 3232
Times Higher Education Supplement	weekly	0171-782 3000
BIOMEDICAL SCIENTISTS		
Nature	weekly	0171-836 6633
BOOK-KEEPERS see also **ACCOUNTING TECHNICIANS**		
Caterer and Hotelkeeper	weekly	0181-652 8380
The Lady	weekly	0171-379 4717
Observer	Sunday	0171-278 2332
Times	Thursday	0171-782 7000
BOOKSELLERS		
Bookseller	weekly	0171-836 8911
Daily Telegraph	Thursday	0171-538 5000
BRAND EXECUTIVES		
Campaign	weekly	0171-413 5479
Marketing	weekly	0171-413 4337

Title	Frequency	Telephone
BRIDGE ENGINEERS		
New Civil Engineer	weekly	0171-938 6000

BROKERS see also FINANCIAL WORKERS, MARKETING EXECUTIVES, SALES EXECUTIVES AND REPRESENTATIVES

Daily Telegraph	Wednesday	0171-538 5000
Guardian	Mon & Sat	0171-278 2332
Independent	Tuesday	0171-253 1222
Independent on Sunday		0171-251 1251
Money Management	weekly	0171-405 6949

BUILDING MANAGEMENT

Construction News	weekly	0171-410 6611
Independent	Thursday	0171-253 1222

BUILDING SERVICES ENGINEERS

Building Services: The CIBSE Journal	monthly	0171-537 2222
Building Services & Environmental Engineer	monthly	0181-340 3291
Caterer and Hotelkeeper	weekly	0181-652 8380
Chartered Builder	monthly	01334 23355
Guardian	Tuesday	0171-278 2332
Jobsearch	weekly	01753 532041
Observer	Sunday	0171-278 2332
Sunday Telegraph		0171-538 5000
Times Higher Education Supplement	weekly	0171-782 3000

BUILDING SERVICES TECHNICIANS

Building Services: The CIBSE Journal	monthly	0171-537 2222

BUILDING SOCIETY MANAGERS

Mortgage Finance Gazette	monthly	0171-538 5386

Title	Frequency	Telephone

BUILDING STUDIES: TEACHERS
Times Educational Supplement	weekly	0171-782 3232
Times Higher Education Supplement	weekly	0171-782 3000

BUILDING SURVEYORS
Building	weekly	0171-537 2222
Chartered Builder	monthly	01344 23355
Health Service Journal	weekly	0171-836 6633
Jobsearch	weekly	01753 532041
Observer	Sunday	0171-278 2332
Sunday Telegraph		0171-538 5000

BURSARS
Daily Telegraph	Thursday	0171-538 5000
Hospitality	monthly	0171-240 4700

BUSINESS ANALYSTS see MANAGEMENT SERVICES OFFICERS

BUSINESS DEVELOPMENT OFFICERS
Guardian	Wednesday	0171-278 2332

BUSINESS STUDIES: TEACHERS
Jobsearch	weekly	01753 532041
Times Educational Supplement	weekly	0171-782 3232

CABIN CREW see also STEWARDS/STEWARDESSES
Daily Mail	Thursday	0171-938 6000
Flight International	weekly	0181-652 3500

CANOEING INSTRUCTORS
Canoe Focus	monthly	01408 496130

CARTOONISTS
Crafts	6 per annum	0171-278 7700
Independent	Wednesday	0171-253 1222

Title	Frequency	Telephone
CATERING MANAGERS		
Caterer and Hotelkeeper	weekly	0181-652 8380
Hospitality	monthly	0171-240 4700
Leisure Week	weekly	0171-494 01300
CERAMICS TECHNICIANS		
Artists Newsletter	monthly	0191-567 3589
CHAMBER STAFF, HOTEL		
Caterer and Hotelkeeper	weekly	0181-652 8380
CHAPLAINS		
Church Times	weekly	0171-359 4570
Methodist Recorder	weekly	0171-251 8414
The Tablet	weekly	0181-748 8484
CHEMICAL ENGINEERS		
Chemical Engineer	weekly	0171-987 6999
Chemistry in Britain	monthly	0171-287 3093
Daily Telegraph	Tues & Thurs	0171-538 5000
Engineer	weekly	0181-855 7777
Jobsearch	weekly	01753 532041
Off-shore Engineer	monthly	0171-987 6999
Sunday Telegraph		0171-538 5000
Sunday Times		0171-782 7000
Times	Thursday	0171-782 7000
Times Higher Education Supplement	weekly	0171-782 3000
CHEMISTS		
Chemical Engineer	weekly	0171-987 6999
Chemistry and Industry	fortnightly	0171-235 3681
Chemistry in Britain	monthly	0171-287 3093
Daily Express	Thursday	0171-928 8000
Daily Telegraph	Thursday	0171-538 5000
Electronics Weekly	weekly	0181-652 3000
Guardian	Tues & Thurs	0171-278 2332
Jobsearch	weekly	01753 532041
Journal: Society of Dyers and Colourists	monthly	01274 725139
New Scientist	weekly	0171-261 2601

Title	Frequency	Telephone
CHEMISTS – *cont.*		
Plastics and Rubber Weekly	weekly	0181-688 7788
Soap, Perfumery and Cosmetics	monthly	013222 77788
Times Educational Supplement	weekly	0171-782 3232
Times Higher Education Supplement	weekly	0171-782 3000
CHOIRMASTERS see also **ORGANISTS AND CHOIRMASTERS**		
Musical Times	monthly	0181-853 2020
CIVIL ENGINEERING TECHNICIANS		
New Civil Engineer	weekly	0171-987 6999
Surveyor	weekly	0171-973 6400
CIVIL ENGINEERS		
Construction News	weekly	0171-410 6611
Daily Express	Thursday	0171-928 8000
Daily Star	Thursday	0171-236 4466
Daily Telegraph	Wed & Thurs	0171-538 5000
Ground Engineering	monthly	0171-987 6999
Guardian	Tuesday	0171-278 2332
Jobsearch	weekly	01753 532041
Sunday Telegraph	weekly	0171-538 5000
Surveyor	weekly	0171-973 6400
Times Educational Supplement	weekly	0171-782 3232
Times Higher Education Supplement	weekly	0171-782 3232
CIVIL ENGINEERING DESIGNERS		
Jobsearch	weekly	01753 532041
Sunday Telegraph	weekly	0171-538 5000
CLERKS OF WORK		
Building	weekly	0171-537 2222

Title	Frequency	Telephone

CLOTHING MANUFACTURERS see also **FASHION BUYERS**
Drapers Record	weekly	0171-404 0429

COMEDIANS
Stage	weekly	0171-403 1818

COMMISSIONING ENGINEERS
Daily Express	Thursday	0171-928 8000
Electrical Review	fortnightly	0181-652 3492
Sunday Telegraph		0171-538 5000

COMMODITY MARKET BROKERS
The Grocer	weekly	01293 613400
Leather	monthly	01732 364422
Metal Bulletin	weekly	0171-827 9977

COMMUNICATIONS ENGINEERS
Jobsearch	weekly	01753 532041

COMMUNITY NURSES see also **NURSES**
Community Outlook	monthly	0171-240 1101

COMPANIONS
The Lady	weekly	0171-379 4717

COMPANY SECRETARIES
Daily Telegraph	Thursday	0171-538 5000
Local Government
  Chronicle	weekly	0171-837 1212
Sunday Telegraph		0171-538 5000
Times	Tuesday	0171-782 7000

COMPUTER OPERATORS
Computer Weekly	weekly	0181-652 3500
Computing	weekly	0171-439 4242
Control and
  Instrumentation	monthly	0181-855 7777
Daily Express	Thursday	0171-928 8000
Daily Telegraph	Mon & Thurs	0171-538 5000

Title	Frequency	Telephone
COMPUTER OPERATORS – *cont.*		
Electronics Weekly	weekly	0181-652 3000
Guardian	Tues, Thurs & Sat	0171-278 2332
Independent	Monday	0171-253 1222
Independent on Sunday		0171-251 1251
Jobsearch	weekly	01753 532041
Opportunities	weekly	0181-667 1667
Sunday Telegraph		0171-538 5000
Sunday Times		0171-782 7000
Surveyor	weekly	0171-333 6400
Times	Thursday	0171-782 7000
Times Educational Supplement	weekly	0171-782 3232
Times Higher Education Supplement	weekly	0171-782 3000
CONFERENCE ORGANISERS		
Caterer and Hotelkeeper	weekly	0181-652 8380
Times	Tuesday	0171-782 7000
CONSUMER PROTECTION		
Opportunities	weekly	0181-667 1667
Guardian	Wednesday	0171-278 2332
CONTRACT ENGINEERS		
Daily Express	Thursday	0171-928 8000
Jobsearch	weekly	01753 532041
CONTRACT MANAGERS		
Building	weekly	0171-537 2222
Chartered Builder	monthly	01344 23355
Construction News	weekly	0171-410 6611
Contract Journal	weekly	0181-652 4642
Daily Star	Thursday	0171-236 4466
Jobsearch	weekly	01753 532041
Sunday Telegraph		0171-538 5000

Title	Frequency	Telephone
COPY WRITERS		
Campaign	weekly	0171-413 5479
Design Week	weekly	0171-439 4222
Marketing	weekly	0171-413 4337
Media Week	weekly	0171-837 1212
COST ACCOUNTANTS see MANAGEMENT ACCOUNTANTS		
COURIERS		
Stage	weekly	0171-403 1818
COURT OFFICIALS		
Justice of the Peace and Local Government Law	weekly	01243 787841
CRYPTOGRAPHERS		
Guardian	Tuesday	0171-278 2332
CURATES		
Church Times	weekly	0171-359 4570
DANCE ADMINISTRATORS		
Guardian	Monday	0171-278 2332
DANCE TEACHERS		
Times Educational Supplement	weekly	0171-782 3232
DANCERS		
Stage	weekly	0171-403 1818
DECKHANDS		
Yachting World	monthly	0171-261 7007
DENTAL HYGIENISTS		
British Dental Journal	fortnightly	0171-387 4499
DENTAL TECHNICIANS		
British Dental Journal	fortnightly	0171-387 4499
Dental Technician	monthly	013727 41411
DENTISTS		
British Dental Journal	fortnightly	0171-387 4499
British Medical Journal	weekly	0171-387 4499

Title	Frequency	Telephone
DESIGNERS		
Campaign	weekly	0171-413 5479
Crafts	6 per annum	0171-278 7700
Creative Review	monthly	0171-439 4222
Daily Mail	Thursday	0171-938 6000
Design Week	weekly	0171-439 4222
Exhibitions Bulletin	monthly	0181-778 2288
Guardian	Mon, Thurs & Sat	0171-278 2332
Marketing	weekly	0171-413 4337
Museums Journal and Recruitment Supplement	monthly	0171-333 1731
Shoe and Leather News	weekly	0181-688 7788
Sunday Times		0171-413 5479
Times	Thursday	0171-782 7000
Times Educational Supplement	weekly	0171-782 3232
Times Higher Education Supplement	weekly	0171-782 3000
XYZ	monthly	0181-943 5034

DETECTIVES see INVESTIGATORS

Title	Frequency	Telephone
DIETICIANS		
Health Service Journal	weekly	0171-836 6633
DIRECT MAIL MANAGERS		
Campaign	weekly	0171-413 5479
Marketing	weekly	0171-413 4337

DISPENSING TECHNICIANS see PHARMACY TECHNICIANS

DISTRICT NURSES see HEALTH VISITORS

Title	Frequency	Telephone
DIVING INSTRUCTORS		
Diver	monthly	0181-943 4288

DOCTORS see MEDICAL DOCTORS

Title	Frequency	Telephone
DRAMA see ACTORS, THEATRE MANAGERS AND PRODUCERS		
Guardian	Saturday	0171-830 7000
Times Educational Supplement	weekly	0171-782 3232

ECOLOGISTS see NATURE CONSERVATIONISTS, WILDLIFE RESERVE MANAGERS

ECONOMISTS

Economist	monthly	0171-830 7000
Estates Gazette	weekly	0171-437 0142
Guardian	Tues & Sat	0171-278 2332
Independent on Sunday		0171-251 1251
Observer	Sunday	0171-278 2332
Planning	weekly	01452 417553
Sunday Times		0171-782 7000
Times	Tues & Thurs	0171-782 7000
Times Educational Supplement	weekly	0171-782 3232
Times Higher Education Supplement	weekly	0171-782 3000

EDITORS

Bookseller	weekly	0171-836 8911
Broadcast	weekly	0171-837 1212
Guardian	Mon & Sat	0171-278 2332
Nature	weekly	0171-836 6633
Sunday Telegraph		0171-538 5000
Times	Tuesday	0171-782 7000
Times Higher Education Supplement	weekly	0171-782 3000

EDUCATION see TEACHERS: PRIMARY AND SECONDARY, TEACHERS: UNIVERSITY AND FURTHER EDUCATION

EFL see ENGLISH TEACHERS: ENGLISH AS A FOREIGN LANGUAGE

Title	Frequency	Telephone
ELECTRICAL ENGINEERING DESIGNERS		
Daily Telegraph	Thursday	0171-538 5000
Jobsearch	weekly	01753 532041
Sunday Telegraph		0171-538 5000
ELECTRICAL ENGINEERING TECHNICIANS		
Jobsearch	weekly	01753 532041
Times Educational Supplement	weekly	0171-782 3232
ELECTRICAL ENGINEERS		
Building	weekly	0171-537 2222
Construction News	weekly	0171-410 6611
Daily Express	Thursday	0171-928 8000
Daily Mail	Thursday	0171-938 6000
Daily Star	Thursday	0171-928 8000
Daily Telegraph	Tues & Thurs	0171-538 5000
Electrical Review	fortnightly	0181-652 3492
Engineer	weekly	0181-855 7777
Guardian	Tues & Sat	0171-278 2332
IEE Recruitment	fortnightly	01438 313311
Jobsearch	weekly	01753 532041
Times Educational Supplement	weekly	0171-782 3232
Times Higher Education Supplement	weekly	0171-782 3000
ELECTRONICS ENGINEERING DESIGNERS		
Electronics World and Wireless World	monthly	0181-652 3500
Jobsearch	weekly	01753 532041
Sunday Telegraph		0171-538 5000
ELECTRONICS ENGINEERS		
Daily Telegraph	Tues & Thurs	0171-538 5000
Electrical Review	fortnightly	0181-652 3492
Electronics Weekly	weekly	0181-652 3000
Guardian	Saturday	0171-278 2332
IEE Recruitment	fortnightly	01438 313311
Jobsearch	weekly	01753 532041

Title	Frequency	Telephone
ELECTRONICS ENGINEERS – *cont.*		
Times Educational Supplement	weekly	0171-782 3232
Times Higher Education Supplement	weekly	0171-782 3000
ELECTRONICS TECHNICIANS		
Control and Instrumentation	monthly	0181-855 7777
Electronics Weekly	weekly	0181-652 3492
Jobsearch	weekly	01753 53204
ENGINEERING DESIGNERS		
Daily Express	Thursday	0171-928 8000
Daily Telegraph	Thursday	0171-538 5000
Jobsearch	weekly	01753 532041
Sunday Telegraph		0171-538 5000
Sunday Times		0171-782 7000
Times	Thursday	0171-782 7000
Times Higher Education Supplement	weekly	0171-782 3000
ENGINEERS		
Building	weekly	0171-537 2222
Control and Instrumentation	monthly	0181-855 7777
Daily Mail	Thursday	0171-938 6000
Daily Telegraph	Tuesday	0171-538 5000
Electrical Review	fortnightly	0181-652 3492
Electronics Weekly	weekly	0181-652 3500
Engineer	weekly	0181-855 7777
Guardian	Tues & Sat	0171-278 2332
Independent	Monday	0171-253 1222
Independent on Sunday		0171-251 1251
Jobsearch	weekly	01753 532041
Municipal Journal	weekly	0171-973 6400
New Scientist	weekly	0171-261 7309
Off-shore Engineer	monthly	0171-987 6999
Opportunities	weekly	0181-667 6000

Title	Frequency	Telephone
ENGINEERS – *cont.*		
Professional Engineering	monthly	01284 763313
Structural Engineer	fortnightly	01778 393313
ENGLISH TEACHERS: ENGLISH AS A FOREIGN LANGUAGE		
EFL Gazette	monthly	0171-937 7534
Guardian	Tuesday	0171-278 2332
Overseas Jobs Express	fortnightly	01273 440220
Times Educational Supplement	weekly	0171-782 3232
ENGLISH TEACHERS: SECONDARY		
Times Educational Supplement	weekly	0171-782 3232
ENGLISH TEACHERS: UNIVERSITY AND FURTHER EDUCATION		
Guardian	Tuesday	0171-278 2332
Times Educational Supplement	weekly	0171-782 3232
Times Higher Education Supplement	weekly	0171-782 3000
ENTERTAINERS		
Stage	weekly	0171-403 1818
ENVIRONMENTAL ENGINEERS see also **BUILDING SERVICES ENGINEERS**		
Chemical Engineer	weekly	0171-987 6999
Water Bulletin	weekly	0171-222 8111
ENVIRONMENTAL HEALTH OFFICERS		
Opportunities	weekly	0181-667 6000
ENVIRONMENTAL SCIENTISTS		
Times Educational Supplement	weekly	0171-782 3232
Water Bulletin	weekly	0171-222 8111
EPIDEMIOLOGISTS		
Guardian	Tues & Wed	0171-278 2332

Title	Frequency	Telephone

ESTATE AGENTS see also SURVEYORS, VALUERS: PROPERTY

Estates Agency News	monthly	01253 722141
Estates Gazette	weekly	0171-437 0142
Estates Times	weekly	0181-855 7777
Times	Tuesday	0171-782 7000

ESTATES MANAGERS

Estates Times	weekly	0181-855 7777
Independent on Sunday	weekly	0171-251 1251
Opportunities	weekly	0181-667 6000

ESTIMATORS: CONSTRUCTION INDUSTRY

Building	weekly	0171-537 2222
Chartered Builder	monthly	01344 23355
Construction News	weekly	0171-410 6611
Daily Telegraph	Tuesday	0171-538 5000
Jobsearch	weekly	01753 532041

ESTIMATORS: PRINTERS

Printing World	weekly	01732 364422

EXHIBITION CO-ORDINATORS

Guardian	Monday	0171-278 2332

EXPORTERS/IMPORTERS

Daily Telegraph	Thursday	0171-538 5000
International Freighting Weekly	weekly	0181-242 3052

FACTORY MANAGERS see WORKS MANAGERS

FARM MANAGERS

Farmers Weekly	weekly	0181-652 4030

FARMERS

Farmers Weekly	weekly	0181-652 4030

FASHION BUYERS

Drapers Record	weekly	0171-404 0429
Fashion Weekly	weekly	0171-404 0431

Title	Frequency	Telephone
FASHION BUYERS – *cont.*		
Independent on Sunday		0171-251 1251
Knitting International	monthly	0171-254 8271
Sunday Times		0171-782 7000
Times	Thursday	0171-782 7000
Times Educational Supplement	weekly	0171-782 3232
Times Higher Education Supplement	weekly	0171-782 3000
FAST FOOD MANAGERS		
Caterer and Hotelkeeper	weekly	0181-652 8380
FILM WORKERS		
Screen International	weekly	0171-837 1212
FINANCIAL WORKERS		
Daily Telegraph	Thursday	0171-538 5000
Economist	monthly	0171-830 7000
Financial Times	Wednesday	0171-873 3000
Guardian	Thursday	0171-278 2332
Independent	Tuesday	0171-253 1222
Independent on Sunday		0171-251 1251
Money Opportunities	weekly	0181-667 1667
Sunday Telegraph		0171-538 5000
FIRE OFFICERS		
Fire	monthly	01737 768611
FISHERMEN AND FISHERIES MANAGERS		
Fishing News	weekly	0171-404 5513

FITNESS INSTRUCTORS see **AEROBICS AND FITNESS INSTRUCTORS**

Title	Frequency	Telephone
FOOD SCIENTISTS		
Food Manufacture	monthly	0181-855 7777
Food Processing	monthly	01732 359990

Title	Frequency	Telephone
FOOD TECHNICIANS		
Food Manufacture	monthly	0181-855 7777
Food Processing	monthly	01732 359990
Opportunities	weekly	0181-667 6000
FORESTERS		
Forestry and British Timber	6 per year	01732 364422
FRANCHISE MANAGERS		
Campaign	weekly	0171-413 5479
Marketing	weekly	0171-413 4337
FREIGHT BUSINESS see EXPORTERS/IMPORTERS		
GENETICISTS		
British Medical Journal	weekly	0171-387 4499
Nature	weekly	0171-836 6633
GEOGRAPHERS		
Estates Times	weekly	0181-855 7777
Guardian	weekly	0171-278 2332
Nature	weekly	0171-836 6633
Planning	weekly	01452 417553
Times Educational Supplement	weekly	0171-782 3232
Times Higher Education Supplement	weekly	0171-782 3000
GEOLOGISTS		
Daily Telegraph	Thursday	0171-538 5000
Ground Engineering	monthly	0171-987 6999
Guardian	Tues & Thurs	0171-278 2332
Nature	weekly	0171-836 6633
New Civil Engineer	weekly	0171-987 6999
New Scientist	weekly	0171-261 7309
Times Educational Supplement	weekly	0171-782 3232
GEOPHYSICISTS		
Nature	weekly	0171-836 6633

Title	Frequency	Telephone
GEOTECHNICAL ENGINEERS		
Chartered Builder	monthly	01334 23355
Daily Telegraph	Thursday	0171-538 5000
Ground Engineering	weekly	0171-987 6999
Jobsearch	weekly	01753 532041
New Civil Engineer	weekly	0171-538 5746
HEALTH AND SAFETY OFFICERS		
Chemical Engineer	weekly	0171-987 6999
Construction News	weekly	0171-410 6611
Daily Telegraph	Thursday	0171-538 5000
Food Manufacture	monthly	0181-855 7777
Jobsearch	weekly	01753 532041
Sunday Telegraph		0171-538 5000
HEALTH PROMOTION OFFICERS		
Health Service Journal	weekly	0171-836 6633
HEALTH VISITORS see also NURSES		
Community Outlook	monthly	0171-240 1101
HEATING AND VENTILATION ENGINEERS see ENVIRONMENTAL ENGINEERS		
HEATING EQUIPMENT TECHNICIANS		
Daily Express	Thursday	0171-928 8000
HIGHWAYS ENGINEERS		
Jobsearch	weekly	01753 532041
New Civil Engineer	weekly	0171-938 6000
HISTORIANS		
Guardian	Tuesday	0171-278 2332
Times Educational Supplement	weekly	0171-728 3232
Times Higher Education Supplement	Tuesday	0171-782 3000

Title	Frequency	Telephone
HOME ECONOMISTS		
Food Manufacture	monthly	0181-855 7777
Times Educational Supplement	weekly	0171-728 3232
Times Higher Education Supplement	weekly	0171-728 3000

HORSES see RIDING INSTRUCTORS, STABLEHANDS

HORTICULTURE		
Grower	weekly	01932 874966
HOTEL AND CATERING MANAGERS		
Caterer and Hotelkeeper	weekly	0181-652 8380
The Lady	weekly	0171-379 4717
Stage	weekly	0171-403 1818
HOUSEKEEPERS		
Catholic Herald	weekly	0171-588 3101
Church Times	weekly	0171-359 4570
The Lady	weekly	0171-379 4717
HOUSEKEEPERS: HOTEL		
Caterer and Hotelkeeper	weekly	0181-652 8380
The Lady	weekly	0171-379 4717
HOUSEMASTERS AND HOUSEMISTRESSES, SCHOOL		
The Lady	weekly	0171-379 4717
HOUSING OFFICERS/MANAGERS		
Estates Gazette	weekly	0171-437 0142
Guardian	Wed & Fri	0171-278 2332
Opportunities	weekly	0181-667 6000
Planning	weekly	01452 417553
HUMAN RESOURCES MANAGERS		
Caterer and Hotelkeeper	weekly	0181-652 8380
Construction News	weekly	0171-410 6611
Daily Telegraph	Thursday	0171-538 5000
Guardian	Tues & Wed	0171-278 2332

Title	Frequency	Telephone

HUMAN RESOURCES MANAGERS – *cont.*
Independent on Sunday   0171-251 1251
Personnel Management monthly 0171-336 7878

ILLUSTRATORS
Guardian Monday 0171-278 2332
Independent Wednesday 0171-253 1222

INDUSTRIAL CHEMISTS
Sunday Telegraph   0171-538 5000

INDUSTRIAL DESIGNERS
Times Educational
 Supplement weekly 0171-782 3232

INDUSTRIAL ENGINEERS
Management Services monthly 0181-363 7452

INDUSTRIAL MANAGERS
Money Management monthly 0171-405 6969

INDUSTRIAL MODELMAKERS
Times Educational
 Supplement weekly 0171-782 3232

INFORMATION OFFICERS see **LIBRARIANS**

INFORMATION SCIENTISTS
Guardian Tues & Sat 0171-278 2332
Library Association
 Record fortnightly 0171-636 7543
New Scientist weekly 0171-261 7309
Times Higher Education
 Supplement weekly 0171-782 3000

INFORMATION TECHNOLOGISTS
Guardian Tuesday 0171-278 2332
Independent Thursday 0171-253 1222
Jobsearch weekly 01753 532041
Times Educational
 Supplement weekly 0171-782 3232

Title	Frequency	Telephone

INSTRUMENT MAINTENANCE
Jobsearch	weekly	01753 532041

INSURANCE AND ASSURANCE AGENTS
Banking World	monthly	0171-388 3171
Daily Express	Tuesday	0171-928 8000
Daily Telegraph	Thursday	0171-538 5000
Lloyds List	Tues & Thurs	0171-250 1500
Money Management	monthly	0171-405 6969
Sunday Telegraph		0171-538 5000

INTERIOR DESIGNERS
Building Design	weekly	0181-855 7777

INTERPRETERS see also TRANSLATORS
Guardian	Wednesday	0171-278 2332
Opportunities	weekly	0181-667 6000

INVESTIGATORS
Daily Telegraph	Thursday	0171-538 5000
Security Gazette	monthly	0181-688 7788

JEWELLERS
Retail Jeweller	monthly	0171-404 2763

JOURNALISTS
Guardian	Mon & Sat	0171-278 2332
UK Press Gazette	weekly	0181-252 3082

KENNELMEN/WOMEN
Horse and Hound	weekly	0171-261 5256

LABORATORY TECHNICIANS
Construction News	weekly	0171-410 6611
Guardian	Saturday	0171-278 2332
Nature	weekly	0171-836 6633
New Scientist	weekly	0171-261 7309

LAND SURVEYORS
Jobsearch	weekly	01753 532041
Surveyor	weekly	0171-973 6400

Title	Frequency	Telephone

LANDSCAPE ARCHITECTS
Landscape Design	monthly	01737 225374
Landscape Design Extra	monthly	01737 225374

LAWYERS
Estates Times	weekly	0181-855 7777
Guardian	Tues & Wed	0171-278 2332
Independent	Thurs	0171-253 1222
Independent on Sunday		0171-251 1251
Law Society Gazette	weekly	0171-242 1222
Lawyer	weekly	0171-287 9800
Local Government Chronicle	weekly	0171-837 1212
Observer	Sunday	0171-278 2332
Opportunities	weekly	0181-667 6000
Times	Tuesday	0171-782 7000
Times Educational Supplement	weekly	0171-782 3232

LEGAL EXECUTIVES
Legal Executive Journal	monthly	01234 860022

LEISURE AND SPORTS CENTRE MANAGERS
Canoe Focus	monthly	01408 496130
Climber and Hill Walker	monthly	013552 46444
Cycling Week	weekly	0171-261 5588
Diver	monthly	0181-943 4288
Golf Club Management	monthly	0121-261 1604
Groundsman	monthly	0171-261 1604
Guardian	Wednesday	0171-278 2332
Horse and Hound	weekly	0171-261 5256
Leisure Opportunities	monthly	01462 431385
Microlight Flying	6 per year	01524 841010
Opportunities	weekly	0181-667 6000
Serve and Volley	6 per year	0171-381 7000
Turf Management	monthly	0181-943 5608

Title	Frequency	Telephone
LIBRARIANS see also INFORMATION SCIENTISTS		
Campaign	weekly	0171-413 5479
Daily Telegraph	Mon & Thurs	0171-538 5000
Guardian	Mon & Wed	0171-278 2332
Health Service Journal	weekly	0171-836 6633
Library Association Record	fortnightly	0171-636 7543
Marketing	weekly	0171-413 4337
Times Higher Education Supplement	weekly	0171-782 3000
LIFE MODELS		
Stage	weekly	0171-403 1818
LIFE SCIENTISTS		
New Scientist	weekly	0171-261 7309
LINGUISTICS		
Guardian	Tuesday	0171-278 2332
LOCAL GOVERNMENT OFFICERS see PUBLIC SECTOR		
MAKE-UP ARTISTS, THEATRICAL		
Times Educational Supplement	weekly	0171-782 3232
MANAGEMENT ACCOUNTANTS		
Health Service Journal	weekly	0171-836 6633
Jobsearch	weekly	01753 532041
Local Government Chronicle	weekly	0171-837 1212
Management Accounting	monthly	0171-637 2311
MANAGEMENT SERVICES OFFICERS (includes Business Analysts, O&M Officers, Work Study Engineers)		
Management Services	monthly	0181-366 1260
MANAGEMENT STUDIES, TEACHERS		
Times Educational Supplement	weekly	0171-782 3000
Times Higher Education Supplement	weekly	0171-782 3000

Title	Frequency	Telephone
MANAGEMENT TRAINERS see also **TRAINING OFFICERS**		
Guardian	Saturday	0171-278 2332
Money Management	monthly	0171-405 6969
Times Higher Education Supplement	weekly	0171-782 3000
MANAGERS/ADMINISTRATORS		
Caterer and Hotelkeeper	weekly	0181-652 8380
Daily Telegraph	Thurs & Sat	0171-436 5000
Economist	monthly	0171-830 7000
Food Manufacture	monthly	0181-855 7777
Guardian	Mon, Thurs, Fri & Sat	0171-278 2332
Health Service Journal	weekly	0171-836 6633
Health Services Management	monthly	0171-240 1101
Independent	Wednesday	0171-253 1222
Independent on Sunday		0171-251 1251
Jobsearch	weekly	01753 532041
Leisure Opportunities	weekly	01462 431385
Local Government Chronicle	weekly	0171-837 1212
Observer	Sunday	0171-278 2332
Printing World	weekly	01732 364422
Retail Week	weekly	0181-688 7788
Sunday Telegraph		0171-538 5000
Sunday Times		0171-782 7000
Times	Mon & Thurs	0171-782 7000
MARINE ENGINEERING TECHNICIANS		
Jobsearch	weekly	01753 532041
MARINE ENGINEERS		
Marine Engineers Review		0171-481 8493
Off-shore Engineer	monthly	0171-987 6999
Sunday Telegraph		0171-538 5000
Yachting World	monthly	0171-261 7007

Title	Frequency	Telephone
MARINE SCIENTISTS		
New Scientist	weekly	0171-261 7309
Times Higher Education Supplement	weekly	0171-782 3000
MARKET ANALYSTS		
Campaign	weekly	0171-413 5479
Guardian	Monday	0171-278 2332
Marketing	weekly	0171-413 4337
MARKET RESEARCHERS		
Campaign	weekly	0171-413 5479
Guardian	Monday	0171-278 2332
Marketing	weekly	0171-413 4337
Observer	weekly	0171-278 2332
MARKETING EXECUTIVES		
Campaign	weekly	0171-413 5479
Caterer and Hotelkeeper	weekly	0181-652 8380
Daily Telegraph		0171-538 5000
Economist	monthly	0171-830 7000
The Grocer	weekly	01293 613400
Guardian	Mon & Sat	0171-278 2332
Independent	Wed & Thurs	0171-253 1222
Marketing	weekly	0171-413 4337
Marketing Week	weekly	0171-439 4222
Sunday Telegraph		0171-538 5000
Sunday Times		0171-782 7000
Times	Thursday	0171-782 7000
Times Higher Education Supplement	weekly	0171-782 3000
MASTERING ENGINEERS		
Music Week	weekly	0171-620 3636

Title	Frequency	Telephone
MATERIALS SCIENTISTS		
Daily Telegraph	Thursday	0171-538 5000
Times Higher Education Supplement	weekly	0171-782 3000
MATHEMATICIANS		
Chemical Engineer	weekly	0171-987 6999
Engineer	weekly	0181-855 7777
Guardian	Tuesday	0171-278 2332
Times Educational Supplement	weekly	0171-782 3000
Times Higher Education Supplement	weekly	0171-782 3000
MATRONS, SCHOOL		
The Lady	weekly	0171-379 4717
Times Educational Supplement	weekly	0171-782 3232
MECHANICAL ENGINEERING DESIGNERS		
Daily Express	Thursday	0171-928 5000
Jobsearch	weekly	01753 532041
Sunday Telegraph		0171-538 5000
MECHANICAL ENGINEERS		
Construction News	weekly	0171-410 6611
Daily Express	Thursday	0171-928 8000
Daily Mail	Thursday	0171-938 6000
Daily Telegraph	Tuesday	0171-538 5000
Engineer	weekly	0181-855 7777
Food Manufacture	monthly	0181-855 7777
Guardian	Tuesday	0171-278 2332
Jobsearch	weekly	01753 532041
Off-shore Engineer	monthly	0171-987 6999
Professional Engineering	monthly	01284 763313
Sunday Telegraph		0171-538 5000
Times	Thursday	0171-782 7000

Title	Frequency	Telephone
MECHANICAL ENGINEERS – *cont.*		
Times Educational Supplement	weekly	0171-782 3232
Times Higher Educational Supplement	weekly	0171-782 3000
MEDIA STUDIES		
Guardian	Mon & Tues	0171-278 2332
Times Educational Supplement	weekly	0171-782 3232
Times Higher Education Supplement	weekly	0171-782 3000
MEDICAL DOCTORS		
British Medical Journal	weekly	0171-387 4499
General Practitioner	weekly	0171-413 4021
Guardian	Wednesday	0171-278 2332
Lancet	weekly	0171-434 4981
Nature	weekly	0171-836 6633
MEDICAL RECEPTIONISTS		
General Practitioner	weekly	0171-413 4021
MEDICAL TECHNICIANS		
Daily Telegraph	Thursday	0171-538 5000
METAL TRADING		
Metal Bulletin	weekly	0171-827 9977
METALLURGISTS		
Daily Express	Thursday	0171-928 8000
MICROBIOLOGISTS		
British Medical Journal	weekly	0171-387 4499
Food Manufacture	monthly	0181-855 7777
Nature	weekly	0171-836 6633
Observer	Sunday	0171-278 2332
Pharmaceutical Journal	weekly	0171-735 9141

Title	Frequency	Telephone
MILITARY ENGINEERS		
Jobsearch	weekly	01753 532041
MINING ENGINEERS see also **GEOTECHNICAL ENGINEERS**		
Mining Journal	weekly	0171-377 2020
MINISTERS OF RELIGION		
Church Times	weekly	0171-359 4570
MUSEUM AND ART GALLERY WORKERS		
Artists Newsletter	monthly	0191-567 3589
Guardian	Monday	0171-278 2332
Museums Journal and Recruitment Supplement	monthly	0171-333 1731
MUSIC RECORDING INDUSTRY		
Music Week	weekly	0171-620 3636
MUSIC TEACHERS: PRIMARY AND SECONDARY		
Classical Music	fortnightly	0171-333 1742
Times Educational Supplement	weekly	0171-782 3232
MUSICIANS		
Classical Music	fortnightly	0171-333 1742
Guardian	Saturday	0171-278 2332
Melody Maker	weekly	0171-261 5519
Musical Times	monthly	0181-836 2020
New Musical Express	weekly	0171-261 5519
Stage	weekly	0171-403 1818
NANNIES		
The Lady	weekly	0171-379 4717
NATURE CONSERVATIONISTS		
Guardian	Friday	0171-278 2332

Title	Frequency	Telephone
NAVAL ARCHITECTS		
Daily Express	Thursday	0171-928 8000
Daily Telegraph	Thursday	0171-538 5000
Jobsearch	weekly	01753 532041
Marine Engineers Review	monthly	0171-481 8493
Naval Architect	monthly	0171-235 4622
Off-shore Engineer	monthly	0171-987 6999
Times Higher Education Supplement	weekly	0171-782 3000
NEUROBIOLOGISTS		
Nature	weekly	0171-836 6633
NUCLEAR ENGINEERS		
Daily Telegraph	Thursday	0171-538 5000
Jobsearch	weekly	01753 532041
NURSES see also HEALTH VISITORS		
General Practitioner	weekly	0171-413 4021
Guardian	Wednesday	0171-278 2332
Jobsearch	weekly	01753 532041
The Lady	weekly	0171-379 4717
Nursing Standard	weekly	0181-423 1066
Nursing Times	weekly	0171-379 0970
Observer	Sunday	0171-278 2332
Times Educational Supplement	weekly	0171-782 3232

ORGANISATION AND METHODS OFFICERS see MANAGEMENT SERVICES OFFICERS

OCCUPATIONAL HEALTH AND SAFETY OFFICERS see HEALTH AND SAFETY OFFICERS

OCCUPATIONAL THERAPISTS		
Church of England Newspaper	weekly	0171-430 2572
Community Care	weekly	0181-642 8870

Title	Frequency	Telephone

OCCUPATIONAL THERAPISTS – *cont.*
Guardian	Wednesday	0171-278 2332
Occupational Health	monthly	0171-407 7541

OFFSHORE OIL AND GAS ENGINEERS
Sunday Telegraph	weekly	0171-538 5000

OPTICAL TECHNICIANS
Optician	weekly	0181-652 8243

OPTICIANS, DISPENSING
Optician	weekly	0181-652 8243

OPTICIANS, OPHTHALMIC
Optician	weekly	0181-652 8243

OPTOMETRISTS
Optician	weekly	0181-652 8243
Optometry Today	fortnightly	01252 816266

ORGANIC CHEMISTS see also **CHEMISTS**
New Scientist	weekly	0171-261 7309

ORGANISTS AND CHOIRMASTERS
Church Times	weekly	0171-359 4570
Musical Times	monthly	0181-836 2020
Times Educational Supplement	weekly	0171-782 3232

OSTEOPATHS
Journal of Alternative and Complementary Medicine	monthly	01932 874333

PACKAGING TECHNOLOGISTS
Daily Telegraph	Thursday	0171-538 5000

PENSIONS MANAGERS
Daily Telegraph	Thursday	0171-538 5000
Money Management	monthly	0171-405 6969
Opportunities	weekly	0181-667 6000
Pensions Management	monthly	0171-363 7452

Title	Frequency	Telephone

PERSONNEL MANAGERS see HUMAN RESOURCES MANAGERS

PHARMACISTS
Chemist and Druggist	weekly	01732 377591
New Scientist	weekly	0171-261 7309
Pharmaceutical Journal	weekly	0171-735 9141

PHARMACOLOGISTS
Nature	weekly	0171-836 6633
Trends in Pharmaceutical Sciences	monthly	01223 315961

PHARMACY TECHNICIANS
Chemist and Druggist	weekly	01732 377591
Nature	weekly	0171-836 6633
Pharmaceutical Journal	weekly	0171-735 9141

PHOTOGRAPHERS
British Journal of Photography	weekly	0171-583 3030
Broadcast	weekly	0171-837 1212
Creative Review	monthly	0171-439 4222
Guardian	Monday	0171-278 2332
Independent	Wednesday	0171-253 1222
Times Educational Supplement	weekly	0171-782 3232
Times Higher Education Supplement	weekly	0171-782 3000
UK Press Gazette	weekly	0181-242 3082

PHOTOGRAPHIC TECHNICIANS
British Journal of Photography	weekly	0171-583 3030

PHYSICAL EDUCATION, TEACHERS
Guardian	Tuesday	0171-278 2332
Times Educational Supplement	weekly	0171-782 3232

Title	Frequency	Telephone

PHYSICISTS
Chemical Engineer	weekly	0171-987 6999
Engineer	weekly	0181-855 7777
IEE Recruitment	fortnightly	01438 313311
Jobsearch	weekly	01753 532041
Nature	weekly	0171-836 6633
Times Educational Supplement	weekly	0171-782 3232
Times Higher Education Supplement	weekly	0171-782 3000

PHYSIOLOGISTS
British Medical Journal	weekly	0171-387 4499
Nature	weekly	0171-836 6633
New Scientist	weekly	0171-938 6000

PHYSIOTHERAPISTS
Leisure Opportunities	weekly	01462 431385
Physiotherapy	monthly	0171-242 1941

PILOTS AND FLIGHT ENGINEERS
Flight International	weekly	0181-652 3500

PIPELINE ENGINEERING DRAUGHTSMEN
Daily Telegraph	Thursday	0171-538 5000

PIPELINE ENGINEERS
Daily Star	Thursday	0171-633 0244
Daily Telegraph	Thursday	0171-538 5000
Jobsearch	weekly	01753 532041
Off-shore Engineer	monthly	0171-987 6999
Sunday Telegraph		0171-538 5000

PLASTICS AND RUBBER INDUSTRY
Plastics and Rubber Weekly	weekly	0181-688 7788

POLICE OFFICERS
Times	Thursday	0171-782 7000

Title	Frequency	Telephone
POLITICAL SCIENTISTS		
Guardian	Tuesday	0171-278 2332
Times Educational Supplement	weekly	0171-782 3232
Times Higher Education Supplement	weekly	0171-782 3000
PONY TREK LEADERS		
The Lady	weekly	0171-379 4717
POWER SYSTEMS ENGINEERS		
Electrical Review	fortnightly	0181-652 3492
POTTERS		
Ceramic Review	fortnightly	0171-439 3377
PRIESTS		
Church Times	weekly	0171-359 4570
PRINTING MANAGERS		
Printing World	weekly	01732 364422
PROBATION OFFICERS		
Guardian	Wednesday	0171-278 3000
PROCESS ENGINEERS		
Chemical Engineer	weekly	0171-987 6999
Daily Telegraph	Tues & Thurs	0171-538 5000
Engineer	weekly	0181-855 7777
Food Manufacture	monthly	0181-855 7777
Jobsearch	weekly	01753 532041
Off-shore Engineer	monthly	0171-987 6999
Sunday Telegraph	weekly	0171-538 5000
Water Bulletin	weekly	0171-222 8111
PRODUCT MANAGERS		
Campaign	weekly	0171-413 5479
Daily Express	Thursday	0171-928 8000
The Grocer	weekly	01293 613400
Marketing	weekly	0171-413 4337

Title	Frequency	Telephone
PRODUCTION ENGINEERS		
Daily Telegraph	Tues & Thurs	0171-538 5000
Jobsearch	weekly	01753 532041
Manufacturing Engineer	monthly	01438 313311
Sunday Telegraph		0171-538 5000
Times Educational Supplement	weekly	0171-782 3232
PRODUCTION MANAGERS		
Drapers Record	weekly	0171-404 0429
Food Manufacture	monthly	0181-855 7777
Plastics and Rubber Weekly	weekly	0181-688 7788
PROJECT MANAGERS/ENGINEERS		
Building	weekly	0171-537 2222
Daily Express	Thursday	0171-928 8000
Jobsearch	weekly	01753 532041
PROPERTY MAKER		
Guardian	Saturday	0171-278 2332
PSYCHIATRISTS		
British Medical Journal	weekly	0171-387 4499
Lancet	weekly	0171-434 4981
PSYCHOLOGISTS		
Guardian	Tues & Wed	0171-278 2332
Times Educational Supplement	weekly	0171-782 3232
Times Higher Education Supplement	weekly	0171-782 3000
PUBLIC HOUSE MANAGERS		
Caterer and Hotelkeeper	weekly	0181-652 8380
PUBLIC RELATIONS OFFICERS see also MARKETING EXECUTIVES		
Campaign	weekly	0171-413 5479
Guardian	Mon & Sat	0171-278 2332
Independent on Sunday		0171-251 1251

Title	Frequency	Telephone

PUBLIC RELATIONS OFFICERS see also MARKETING EXECUTIVES – *cont.*

Marketing	weekly	0171-413 4337
PR Week	weekly	0171-413 4543

PUBLIC SECTOR

Guardian	Wednesday	0171-278 2332
Health Service Journal	weekly	0171-836 6633
Independent	Thursday	0171-253 1222
Jobsearch	weekly	01753 532041
Leisure Opportunities	weekly	01462 431385
Museums Journal and Recruitment Supplement	monthly	0171-333 1731
Opportunities	weekly	0181-667 6000
Planning	weekly	01452 417553
Public Finance and Accountancy	weekly	0171-895 8823

PUBLISHING

Bookseller	weekly	0171-836 8911
Guardian	Mon & Sat	0171-278 2332
Media Week	weekly	0181-688 7788

PURCHASING OFFICERS

Daily Telegraph	Thursday	0171-538 5000
Drapers Record	weekly	0171-404 0429
Health Service Journal	weekly	0171-836 6633
Printing World	weekly	01732 364422
Procurement Weekly	weekly	01643 261262
Sunday Times		0171-782 7000
Times	Thursday	0171-782 7000

QUALITY CONTROL ENGINEERS

Daily Telegraph	Thursday	0171-538 5000
Jobsearch	weekly	01753 532041
Sunday Telegraph		0171-538 5000

Title	Frequency	Telephone
QUALITY CONTROLLERS		
Drapers Record	weekly	0171-404 0429
Food Manufacture	monthly	0181-855 7777
Jobsearch	weekly	01753 532041
Pharmaceutical Journal	weekly	0171-735 9141
QUANTITY SURVEYORS		
Building	weekly	0171-537 2222
Chartered Builder	monthly	01344 23355
Construction News	weekly	0171-410 6611
Daily Telegraph	Thursday	0171-538 5000
Jobsearch	weekly	01753 532041
QUARRYING INDUSTRY		
Quarry Management		01602 411315
RADIO see TELEVISION AND RADIO		
RADIOGRAPHERS		
Guardian	Tuesday	0171-278 2332
Times Higher Education Supplement	weekly	0171-782 3000
RECEPTIONISTS see also MEDICAL RECEPTIONISTS		
Jobsearch	weekly	01753 532041
Times	Monday	0171-782 7000
RECEPTIONISTS, HOTEL		
Caterer and Hotelkeeper	weekly	0181-652 8380
RECREATION MANAGERS		
Leisure Opportunities	weekly	01462 431385
RECRUITMENT CONSULTANTS		
Daily Telegraph	Thursday	0171-538 5000
REFRIGERATION AND AIR CONDITIONING ENGINEERS see also ENVIRONMENTAL ENGINEERS		
Refrigeration and Air Conditioning	monthly	0181-688 7788

Title	Frequency	Telephone
RELIGION: TEACHERS		
The Tablet	weekly	0181-748 8484
Times Educational Supplement	weekly	0171-782 3232
REPORTERS		
Guardian	Monday	0171-278 2332
RESEARCH AND DEVELOPMENT		
Times Higher Education Supplement	weekly	0171-782 3000
RESEARCHERS		
Guardian	Saturday	0171-278 2332
RESTAURANT MANAGERS see also CATERING MANAGERS, FAST FOOD MANAGERS		
Caterer and Hotelkeeper	weekly	0181-652 8380
Daily Express	Tuesday	0171-982 8000
Jobsearch	weekly	01753 532041
RETAILING see also STORE MANAGERS		
Daily Express	Tuesday	0171-928 8000
The Grocer	weekly	01293 613400
Guardian	Thursday	0171-278 2332
Independent on Sunday		0171-251 1251
RIDING INSTRUCTORS		
Horse and Hound	weekly	0171-261 5256
SAILING INSTRUCTORS		
Canoe Focus	monthly	01408 496130
SALES EXECUTIVES AND REPRESENTATIVES see also FINANCIAL WORKERS, INSURANCE AND ASSURANCE AGENTS, MARKETING EXECUTIVES		
Autocar and Motor	weekly	0181-943 5000
British Journal of Photography	weekly	0171-583 3030
Cabinet Maker	weekly	01732 364422
Caterer and Hotelkeeper	weekly	0181-652 8380
Construction News	weekly	0171-410 6611

Title	Frequency	Telephone
SALES EXECUTIVES AND REPRESENTATIVES – *cont.*		
Cycling Week	weekly	0171-261 5588
Daily Express	Tues, Wed & Thurs	0171-928 8000
Daily Mail	Tues & Thurs	0171-938 6000
Daily Star	Thursday	0171-928 8000
Daily Telegraph	Thurs & Sat	0171-538 5000
Drapers Record	weekly	0171-404 0429
Electronics Weekly	weekly	0181-652 3000
Engineer	weekly	0181-855 7777
Farmers Weekly	weekly	0181-652 4030
Flight International	weekly	0181-652 3500
The Grocer	weekly	01293 613400
Guardian	Mon, Fri & Sat	0171-278 2332
Independent	Wednesday	0171-253 1222
Jobsearch	weekly	01753 532041
Media Week	weekly	0181-688 7788
Menswear	weekly	0181-688 7788
Money Management	monthly	0171-405 6969
Observer	Sunday	0171-278 2332
Packaging News	monthly	0181-242 3157
Packaging Week	weekly	01732 364422
Printing World	weekly	01732 364422
Refrigeration and Air Conditioning	monthly	0181-688 7788
Stage	weekly	0171-403 1818
Sunday Times		0171-782 7000
Times	Wed & Thurs	0171-782 7000
SANDWICH DELIVERERS		
Stage	weekly	0171-403 1818
SANITARY ENGINEERS		
Daily Telegraph	Tuesday	0171-538 5000
Jobsearch	weekly	01753 532041
SCHOOLS EXAMINERS		
Times Educational Supplement		0171-782 3232

Title	Frequency	Telephone
SCIENCE TEACHERS, SECONDARY		
Times Educational Supplement	weekly	0171-782 3232
SCIENTISTS		
Daily Express	Thursday	0171-928 8000
Daily Telegraph	Thursday	0171-538 5000
Economist	monthly	0171-830 7000
Guardian	Tues & Thurs	0171-278 2332
Independent	Monday	0171-253 1222
Independent on Sunday		0171-251 1251
Nature	weekly	0171-836 6633
New Scientist		0171-261 7309
Opportunities	weekly	0181-667 6000
Sunday Times	weekly	0171-782 7000
Times	Thursday	0171-782 7000
Times Educational Supplement	weekly	0171-782 3232
Times Higher Education Supplement	weekly	0171-782 3000
SCULPTORS		
Artists Newsletter	monthly	0191-567 3589
Arts Management Weekly	weekly	0171-333 1733
Guardian	Monday	0171-278 2332
SECRETARIES		
Campaign	weekly	0171-413 5479
Church Times	weekly	0171-359 4570
Daily Telegraph	Thursday	0171-538 5000
Guardian	Mon, Wed & Sat	0171-278 2332
Health Service Journal	weekly	0171-836 6633
Independent	Thursday	0171-253 1222
Independent on Sunday		0171-251 1251
Jobsearch	weekly	01753 532041
Times	Mon, Tues & Thurs	0171-782 7000

Title	Frequency	Telephone
SERVICE ENGINEERS		
Jobsearch	weekly	01753 532041
SINGERS		
Classical Music	fortnightly	0171-333 1742
Melody Maker	weekly	0171-261 5519
Stage	weekly	0171-403 1818
SITE AGENTS		
Chartered Builder	monthly	01344 23355
Construction News	weekly	0171-410 6611
SOCIAL WORKERS		
Church Times	weekly	0171-359 4570
Community Care	weekly	0171-837 1212
Disability Now	monthly	0171-251 1362
Guardian	Tues & Sat	0171-278 2332
Jobsearch	weekly	01753 532041
Local Government Chronicle	weekly	0171-837 1212
Methodist Recorder	weekly	0171-251 8414
Opportunities	weekly	0181-667 6000
Time Out	weekly	0171-813 6004
Times Educational Supplement	weekly	0171-782 3232
Times Higher Education Supplement	weekly	0171-782 3000

SOLICITORS see LAWYERS

Title	Frequency	Telephone
SONG WRITERS		
Melody Maker	weekly	0171-261 5519

SPORT see LEISURE AND SPORTS CENTRE MANAGERS

Title	Frequency	Telephone
SPORTS SCIENTISTS		
Times Higher Education Supplement	weekly	0171-782 3000

Title	Frequency	Telephone
STABLEHANDS		
Horse and Hound	weekly	0171-261 5256
STATISTICIANS		
Guardian	Tues & Sat	0171-278 2332
Health Service Journal	weekly	0171-836 6633
New Scientist	weekly	0171-261 7309
Times Educational Supplement	weekly	0171-782 3232
STEWARDS/STEWARDESSES		
Yachting World	monthly	0171-261 7007
STOCK CONTROLLERS		
Autocar and Motor	weekly	0181-943 5000
Sunday Telegraph		0171-538 5000
STORE MANAGERS		
Daily Express	Tuesday	0171-928 8000
Daily Mail	Thursday	0171-938 6000
Daily Telegraph	Thursday	0171-538 5000
Fish Trader	fortnightly	01737 768611
The Grocer	weekly	01293 613400
Jobsearch	weekly	01753 532041
Times	Thursday	0171-782 7000
STRUCTURAL ENGINEERS		
Daily Telegraph	Thursday	0171-538 5000
Ground Engineering	monthly	0171-987 6999
Jobsearch	weekly	01753 532041
Off-shore Engineer	monthly	0171-987 6999
Sunday Telegraph		0171-538 5000
Times Higher Education Supplement	weekly	0171-782 3000
STUDIO MANAGERS		
Music Week	weekly	0171-620 3636
SUBSEA ENGINEERS		
Off-shore Engineer	monthly	0171-987 6999

Title	Frequency	Telephone
SURVEYORS		
Building	weekly	0171-537 2222
Estates Gazette	weekly	0171-437 0142
Estates Times	weekly	0181-855 7777
Opportunities	weekly	0181-667 6000
Planning	weekly	01452 417553
Surveyor	weekly	0171-973 6400
SWIMMING INSTRUCTORS		
Swimming Times	monthly	01509 234433
TAXATION see ACCOUNTANTS		
TEACHERS: MODERN LANGUAGES see also		
INTERPRETERS, TRANSLATORS		
Guardian	Tues & Wed	0171-278 2332
Times Educational Supplement	weekly	0171-782 3232
Times Higher Education Supplement	weekly	0171-782 3000
TEACHERS: NURSERY		
Times Educational Supplement	weekly	0171-782 3232
TEACHERS: PRIMARY AND SECONDARY		
Church of England Newspaper	weekly	0171-490 01896
Church Times	weekly	0171-359 4570
Classical Music	fortnightly	0171-333 1742
Guardian	Tuesday	0171-278 2332
Observer	Sunday	0171-278 2332
The Tablet	weekly	0181-748 8484
Times	Monday	0171-782 7000
Times Educational Supplement	weekly	0171-782 3232
The Universe	weekly	0161-236 8856
TEACHERS: UNIVERSITY AND FURTHER EDUCATION		
British Medical Journal	weekly	0171-387 4499
Building Services: The CIBSE Journal	monthly	0171-537 2222

Title	Frequency	Telephone
TEACHERS: UNIVERSITY AND FURTHER EDUCATION – *cont.*		
Chemical Engineer	weekly	0171-987 6999
Chemistry and Industry	fortnightly	0171-235 3681
Chemistry in Britain	monthly	0171-287 3093
Classical Music	fortnightly	0171-333 1742
Community Care	weekly	0171-837 1212
Computer Weekly	weekly	0181-652 3500
Computing	weekly	0171-439 4242
Guardian	Tuesday	0171-278 2332
Independent	Thursday	0171-253 1222
Jobsearch	weekly	01753 532041
Nature	weekly	0171-836 6633
New Civil Engineer	weekly	0171-987 6999
Times Educational Supplement	weekly	0171-782 3232
Times Higher Education Supplement	weekly	0171-782 3000
TECHNICAL AUTHORS		
Jobsearch	weekly	01753 532041
Sunday Telegraph		0171-538 5000
TECHNOLOGY TEACHERS		
Times Educational Supplement	weekly	0171-782 3232
TELECOMMUNICATIONS ENGINEERS		
Jobsearch	weekly	01753 532041
Sunday Telegraph		0171-538 5000
TELEMETRY ENGINEERS		
Control and Instrumentation	monthly	0181-855 7777
TELEVISION AND RADIO		
Broadcast	weekly	0171-837 1212
Guardian	Mon & Sat	0171-278 2332
TELEVISION ENGINEERS		
Broadcast	weekly	0171-837 1212

Title	Frequency	Telephone
TENNIS COACHES		
Serve and Volley	6 per annum	0171-381 7000
TEXTILE DESIGNERS		
Times Educational Supplement	weekly	0171-782 3232
THEATRE MANAGERS AND PRODUCERS		
Arts Management Weekly	weekly	0171-333 1733
Guardian	Mon, Tues & Sat	0171-278 2332
Stage	weekly	0171-403 1818
TIMBER TECHNOLOGISTS		
Times Higher Education Supplement	weekly	0171-782 3000

TOURISM see **TRAVEL AND TOURISM CONSULTANTS**

Title	Frequency	Telephone
TOWN AND COUNTRY PLANNERS		
Guardian	Wed & Fri	0171-278 2332
TOWN CLERKS		
Local Government Chronicle	weekly	0171-837 1212
TRADE UNIONS AND INDUSTRIAL RELATIONS OFFICERS		
Morning Star	daily	0171-254 01033
Tribune	weekly	0171-278 01911
TRADING STANDARDS OFFICERS		
Building	weekly	0171-537 2222
TRAFFIC MANAGERS AND CONTROLLERS		
Jobsearch	weekly	01753 532041
New Civil Engineer	weekly	0171-987 6999
Surveyor	weekly	0171-973 6400
Traffic Engineering and Control	monthly	0171-636 3956

Title	Frequency	Telephone

TRAINING OFFICERS see also MANAGEMENT TRAINERS

Guardian	Mon, Tues, Wed & Thurs	0171-278 2332
Health Service Journal	weekly	0171-836 6633
Jobsearch	weekly	01753 532041
Personnel Management	monthly	0171-336 7878
Times Higher Education Supplement	weekly	0171-782 3000
Training and Development	monthly	01502 575660

TRANSLATORS see also INTERPRETERS

Guardian	Mon, Wed & Fri	0171-278 2332
Independent	Thursday	0171-253 1222
Linguist	monthly	0171-359 7445
Sunday Telegraph	weekly	0171-538 5000

TRANSPORT MANAGERS

The Grocer	weekly	01293 613400
Observer	Sunday	0171-278 2332
Transport	6 per annum	01494 678000

TRANSPORT STUDIES

Times Higher Education Supplement	weekly	0171-782 3000

TRAVEL AND TOURISM CONSULTANTS

Jobsearch	weekly	01753 532041
Times Educational Supplement	weekly	0171-782 3232
Travel Trade Gazette	weekly	01732 362666
Travel Weekly	weekly	0171-359 7445

VALUERS: PROPERTY

Estates Gazette	weekly	0171-437 0142
Planning	weekly	01452 417553

VETERINARY NURSES

Veterinary Record	weekly	0171-636 6541

Title	Frequency	Telephone
VETERINARY SURGEONS		
Farmers Weekly	weekly	0181-652 4030
Nature	weekly	0171-836 6633
Veterinary Record	weekly	0171-636 6541
VICARS		
Church Times	weekly	0171-359 4570
VIDEO MAKERS		
Times Higher Education Supplement	weekly	0171-782 3000
WARDROBE STAFF: THEATRE		
Stage	weekly	0171-403 1818
WASTES MANAGEMENT WORKERS		
Surveyor	weekly	0171-973 6400
Wastes Management	monthly	01604 20426
WATER ENGINEERS		
New Civil Engineer	weekly	0171-987 6999
Water Bulletin	weekly	0171-222 8111
WILDLIFE RESERVE MANAGERS		
Guardian	Friday	0171-278 2332
WORK STUDY ENGINEERS see MANAGEMENT SERVICES OFFICERS		
WORKS MANAGERS		
Food Manufacture	monthly	0181-855 7777
Health Service Journal	weekly	0171-836 6633
Poultry World	weekly	0181-652 4025
Printing World	weekly	01732 364422
Sunday Telegraph	weekly	0171-538 5000
ZOOLOGISTS		
Nature	weekly	0171-836 6633
Science	weekly	01223 302067

GNVQ: is it for you?

The Guide to General National Vocational Qualifications and general SVQs, the Scottish equivalent (age 14+)

This paperback shows students what it would really be like to study for a GNVQ/General SVQ.

Interviews with students on the pilot schemes give the flavour of assignment work in all its variety. The book gives tips on managing an open-ended workload, building a portfolio of evidence and getting on with colleagues in team projects. It takes students through all the subjects on offer and puts the case for and against combining a GNVQ/General SVQ with another qualification such as an A-level. Last but not least, it offers a realistic assessment of the work and higher education opportunities that will follow.

GNVQ: is it for you? is an ideal starting point for anyone considering GNVQs/General SVQs.

Author Windsor Chorlton
Foreword by Gilbert Jessup, Deputy Chief Executive, NCVQ
Publication March 1994
Format 198 x 126mm, 192pp, paperback

To order, phone **0403 710851**
If you have any queries, phone **0223 464334**

Your Choice of A-levels

The essential guide to A-level and AS subjects and examinations (age 14 –16)

Listed as part of the Government's Careers Library Initiative

Essential reading for all students (and their parents) who are considering AS/A-levels.

Over 40 AS and A-level subjects are analysed by a team of A-level teachers and examiners. The opening chapters give an overview of the move from GCSEs to A-levels. Subject chapters explain what is expected of students and what students can expect.

Includes the latest information on course content and combinations of subjects; teaching and learning methods; examinations and assessment; entry into higher education and careers; and a full listing of approved AS subjects. Also covers alternatives such as BTEC, GNVQ/General SVQ and the International Baccalaureate.

> *'... an excellent guide to all aspects of A-level work including information on AS.'*

Times Educational Supplement

Authors Mary Munro & Alan Jamieson
Publication November 1993
Format 198 x 126mm, 334pp,

Decisions at 17/18+

Your options at 18: higher education, work, a year out (age 16–18)

Listed as part of the Government's Careers Library Initiative

Designed with the school- and college-leaver in mind, this completely revised edition helps the student to look forward into the next decade, as well as to examine what is on offer in the immediate future. It attempts to weigh up the options available after the sixth form and show where chosen subjects might lead.

Decisions at 17/18+ shows students how to examine both their own talents and the needs of the fast-changing world of work – and hence to select the most promising career routes. The new edition includes updates on the many changes in higher education and training, including information on the 'new' universities. It also covers the jobs open to students who want to work at 18.

Unpatronising text allied with diagrams and cartoons make this an essential read for the whole range of students now staying on in education to 18.

Includes: • staying on for a third year at sixth form • moving to higher education • going to work • starting on a sandwich course • and taking a year off.

Authors Michael Smith & Veronica Matthew
Publication October 1993
Format 198 x 126mm, 208pp, paperback

CVs and Applications
How to present yourself on paper (age 16+)

CVs and Applications explores all the ins and outs of university/college and job applications, writing a dazzling CV and covering letter, and generally presenting oneself well on paper. This new *Helpbook* provides examples of different CV layouts, application forms and letters, and deals specifically with common problems and mistakes. Using checklists, exercises and practical tips the reader creates his or her own 'selling points' and follows the sympathetic step-by-step guide to completing an application.

An invaluable and practical guide for anyone wishing to paint themselves in the best possible light.

Includes the latest advice on how to complete the UCAS form.

Author Patricia McBride
Publication February 1994
Format 198 x 126mm, 182pp, paperback

Student Life: A Survival Guide

(age 17+)

Student Life is a survival guide for anyone about to enter university or colleges in their first year or just thinking about it. Its lively style offers practical advice, anecdotes and interviews with students on issues close to a student's heart.

Includes: • where to live • how to conserve cash • keeping up with studies • making friends • staying healthy • and keeping out of trouble

Students can't leave home without it!

'Student Life *should be made compulsory reading for all those about to enter the higher education system.*'
Dr T Stone, University Senior Tutor, University of Warwick

Author Natasha Roe
Publication April 1994
Format 198 x 126mm, 198pp, paperback

Decisions at 13/14+

The starting point for GCSE options (age 13→16)

Listed as part of the Government's Careers Library Initiative

Students need the right information to choose the right GCSE courses. For many it is their first experience of making decisions which will affect their future. *Decisions at 13/14+* begins with a detailed step-by-step guide to decision-making and it goes on to give information on every subject students are likely to encounter. It also encourages forward thinking by pointing the way to academic options after school and includes an A–Z look at areas of work. The 1994 edition covers the changes resulting from Sir Ron Dearing's review of the National Curriculum, as well as updates on areas of work and the qualifications needed to enter them.

> *'I would, and will, urge every Year 9 pupil to persuade their parents to buy one.'*

Ken Hulme, Newscheck

> *'When a book has been in print in many editions for over 20 years, it's a fair guide to its usefulness.'*

Lifeforce

Authors Veronica Matthew & Michael Smith
Publication March 1994
Format 198 x 126mm, 318pp, paperback